The New Landlord's Handbook

Definitive Strategies for Successful Rental Property
Management for first-time Landlords

Donald E. Clay

Copyright

The New Landlord's Handbook

Contents

Introduction

For new investors, navigating rental property management can be overwhelming. There's a lot to learn, from finding the right tenant and writing your lease to filing taxes at the end of the year. This is why some investors choose to commit their rental properties to third-party management organizations. However, for those looking to optimize profits and are prepared to do some administrative work, managing your own rental property can not only teach you vital lessons that will help you expand your real estate business, but it will also allow you to streamline operations and enhance ROI. Real estate investment has generally been a pretty safe long-term approach for wealth accumulation, and your plan is to purchase multiple properties and run them yourself. However, what would it take to buy and retain these investments while ensuring that they generate a profit over time?

Even during prosperous economic times, keeping a portfolio of profitable assets requires time, effort, and money. Owning an income property usually entails being available at any moment in case of an emergency. Having the right mentality and perspectives determines whether a property owner succeeds or fails in keeping and managing properties. A successful real estate management approach requires patience, responsiveness, and communication skills.

The capacity to plan is equally critical for long-term success. Creating a long-term plan will help you identify your goals and objectives while also managing your progress. A strong plan serves as a reminder of where you're going and how you'll get there. The first step toward a career in property management is self-analysis. Before investing in property management, you must first determine whether you are willing to commit to a long-term strategy. What is your temperament?
Can you handle emergencies or financial difficulties? Are you an excellent judge of character, able to identify troublesome potential renters? These and other concerns should be addressed to ensure that you can handle any rental situation.

Becoming a property owner entails six basic disciplines that require skills and knowledge.

Sales and Marketing	Ability to promote and advertise to potential tenants. The ability to efficiently sell property.

Money Management	Able to comprehend and handle finances. Knowing when and how to boost your revenue.
Building structure and Carpentry	Understand fundamental carpentry, electrical, plumbing, and temperature control systems. Understand the property's characteristics, landscape, and building inspection standards.
Communication	Ability to interact with maintenance and repair staff, municipal officials, and tenants.
Negotiation	Capable of negotiating prices, terms, and conditions, among other things. Capable of dealing with both tenants and property sellers.
Regulatory	Understanding of building codes, zoning, and other regulations. Understand the permit requirements and process.

Once you've determined that you have the potential to become a property owner, you'll want to learn about the challenges associated with property management. The table above demonstrates how numerous disciplines connect when you own and manage real estate. Running a property will become easier after you understand each discipline and devise a strategy to deal with components inside each discipline. Let's look at the fundamentals of income property management.

- *Finding the right property* - Searching for sturdy properties with high rental potential; what to check for during an inspection; and how to calculate revenue and expenses.
- *Buying the property* - How to negotiate a favorable price, terms, and other considerations; what sort of mortgage to use and when to renew; and when to employ creative financing to purchase the home.
- *Attracting and maintaining tenants* - How to bring in tenants, keep them happy, and make money from them; knowing which channels to utilize to recruit the best tenants; and when to enhance rental income.
- *Resolving building and property issues* - Handling repairs, equipment replacement, code violations, weather damage, and updates; interacting with neighbors and community members; adhering to regulations and requirements.
- *Handling tenant difficulties* - How to handle damaged property, missed payments, community violations (unsafe conditions, loud noise), occupancy violations, and other lease difficulties, including special requests.
- *Dealing with vacancies* - Limiting unoccupied space; boosting rental opportunities; and preventing vacancies through long-term relationships.
- *Financial activities* - Settling expenses such as repairs, maintenance, upgrading, and waste removal; settling

property debts; and timely collection of rental pay-ments.

You do not need to be an expert in every facet of property management; but, becoming familiar with each one will increase your chances of success and reduce your headaches. Remember, if you want to stay in this field for a long while, you'll be better off if you take the time to learn more.

CHAPTER ONE
THE ROLE OF A LANDLORD

Who is a Landlord?

Anyone who owns real estate and leases it to a third party in exchange for rent is referred to as a landlord. Landlords might be persons, businesses, or other organizations. Typically, landlords perform required maintenance or repairs throughout the rental period, while tenants or leaseholders are responsible for the property's cleanliness and general care. A lease agreement typically defines each party's specific duties and obligations.

As previously said, a landlord is someone who owns property and rents it out to others. This party is known as the renter or leaseholder. Landlords invest in real estate to generate a profit. A landlord can receive a consistent stream of revenue while also increasing the value of their property. Landlords can be persons, businesses, or other institutions, such as governments. Similarly, the types of properties they possess may vary. That suggests they own more than just homes. In addition to single-family dwellings, their real estate portfolios could include:

- Multi-family residential dwellings, such as multifamily residences, apartment complexes, and condominiums

- Land and empty spaces.
- Vacation properties, including cottages and villas
- Commercial assets include standalone businesses, shopping malls, office complexes, and mixed-use structures.

Landlords frequently employ leases to rent out their assets. A lease is a legally binding contract that sets forth the terms under which one party agrees to rent property from another. It assures the lessee or renter the use of an asset while also ensuring that the lessor (the property owner or landlord) receives regular payments for a predetermined period of time in exchange.

Landlords must comply with certain legal duties, such as keeping the rental unit fit for habitation, in order to keep their premises livable and safe. They collect rent to compensate housing renters and may charge late fees if payments are not paid on time. Landlords' responsibilities go beyond simply collecting rent; they must also strictly adhere to fair housing legislation and respect lease agreements with tenants. Landlords cannot force tenants to give up certain rights through lease stipulations; such safeguards are necessary to ensure healthy landlord-tenant relationships.

Land Rights and Responsibilities

Landlords' rights and responsibilities differ by state, however there are core regulations that apply to all jurisdictions.

Property owners have the right to collect rent and any pre-arranged late fines. They also have the power to increase the rent as specified in the tenant-landlord lease agreement. When tenants do not pay their rent, landlords have the power to evict them. The process of eviction differs by state. Most states allow landlords to collect both back rent and legal costs.

Property owners must:

- Responsible for keeping their rental units in habitable condition.
- Managing Security Deposits
- Ensure a property is tidy and unoccupied when a new renter moves in.
  The landlord must also adhere to all local construction codes, make timely repairs, and keep all critical amenities, such as electricity, plumbing, and heat, operational.
- The tenancy must be registered within one month of its start date.
- Issue tenants a rent book, statement, or receipt attesting to the payments they have made for rent and any additional sums (such utilities) that the landlord has received.
- Ensure that the property conforms with minimum standards legislation
- Keep the property in the condition it was in at the commencement of the tenancy.
- Pay back the tenants for any repairs they made after requesting them from the landlord and the landlord

failing to do so in a timely manner. The laws governing landlord-tenant relationships differ by state. In general, a landlord has three to seven days to address serious issues (such as no heat or running water) and 30 days for less severe problems.

o Insure the property. (A landlord is required to keep insurance solely for the structural dwelling, i.e. bricks and mortar). A tenant should obtain contents insurance to protect their personal items.

o Pay any extra fees or taxes related to the property that the tenant is not liable for.

o Provide contact information for the tenant (or the agent operating on behalf of the landlord).

o Terminate the tenancy in accordance with legislation. Unless legitimately withheld, the tenant's deposit must be returned immediately at the end of the tenancy. A landlord may deduct rent arrears, outstanding bills, or the cost of repairs to the dwelling that exceed reasonable wear and tear. If a tenant ends a tenancy early, the landlord can deduct the losses incurred.

o Schedule a property inspection. Landlords are advised to conduct frequent inspections of their property.

Limits on a Landlord's Right

Here are four major things landlords are restricted from doing:

o *Discriminate* - The Fair Housing Act prohibits landlords from denying a lease to anyone based on their color, race, sexual orientation, national origin, disability, familial status, or gender.

- o *Enter without proper notice* - Unless there is an emergency, such as a fire or a leak, landlords must give sufficient notice before accessing a property. Although state laws differ, many statutes demand at least 24 hours' notice.
- o *Evict tenants improperly* - A landlord may evict a tenant for a variety of reasons, but they must always follow the necessary legal procedures. Failure to follow basic protocol places the landlord in a dangerous legal situation.
- o *Rent raise without notice* - Landlords must provide enough notice before raising a tenant's rent (usually 30 days). Additionally, rent control regulations may prohibit landlords from raising rates above a particular threshold in some states, even in situations where a lease's renewal is imminent.

Fair Housing Laws

As a property manager or landlord, you must understand the importance of following all applicable laws. This includes eviction laws, landlord-tenant legislation, and civil laws in general. However, there is another crucial set of rules: *fair housing laws*. These housing rules govern many elements of a landlord's business, therefore it is critical to be conversant with them.

So, in the next few paragraphs, we'll go over what they are, how they might be violated, and how to avoid them. To begin, let us look at the Fair Housing Act, which is where it all began.

What is the Fair Housing Act?

The Fair Housing Act, passed as part of the Civil Rights Act of 1968, is an important piece of legislation. It was created to protect individuals from housing discrimination, and it includes a broad variety of protected classifications such as race, religion, national origin, and handicap. The Fair Housing Act's principal purpose is to make sure that everybody is given equal chances to live in their preferred community. This means that landlords and property owners may not discriminate against interested tenants or buyers on the basis of their protected class. Federal Fair Housing Laws were produced as a result of the Fair Housing Act and are designed to uphold the act. We'll go over the act's Fair Housing Laws in further detail below.

What are Fair Housing Laws?

Fair housing laws are a set of legislation aimed at protecting individuals from housing discrimination. These regulations apply to all sorts of housing, including rents, sales, and mortgages, and they protect a wide spectrum of groups, as we will see below.

Fair housing rules apply throughout the housing process, including advertising, displaying houses, and negotiating lease or sale conditions. This means that landlords and property owners cannot market their properties in ways that discriminate against specific categories of individuals.

Landlords must also evaluate their local fair housing legislation to ensure compliance. Below, we mentioned protected classes. Landlords must be conversant with these protected classifications to ensure that they do not violate the law. The Fair Housing Act's protected classifications will be discussed in detail below:

The Protected Class

A feature of any person who is shielded from discrimination by the Fair Housing Laws is considered a protected class under the Fair Housing Act. Thus, to put it simply, discrimination on the basis of these protected classes is prohibited for landlords and property managers:

- Religion
- Race
- Sex
- Color

- National origin
- Disability
- Familial status

This means that all of these classifications are protected under the Fair Housing Laws, and discrimination based on them is a serious offense. Thus, while we have discussed the nature of laws and the people they protect extensively, we have not covered the ways in which they are broken.

Common Fair Housing Law Violations

To prevent tenant discrimination, landlords must understand and follow fair housing regulations. Violating these regulations can result in serious penalties, such as fines and legal action. Here are some frequent methods for landlords to violate fair housing laws:

- *Refusing to rent an* **individual** – It is prohibited for landlords to refuse to rent to someone based on their race, color, national origin, gender, religion, disability, or familial status. This involves using language in rental property advertisements that expresses favoritism or hostility toward particular demographic groups.
- **Treating tenants differently** – Landlords are not permitted to discriminate against tenants based on race, religion, or any other protected feature. A landlord, for example, may refuse to rent a more desirable flat to a tenant of a particular religion or race.
- **Asking prohibited questions** – Landlords are not permitted to inquire about a prospective tenant's race,

national origin, family status, or religion during the lease application process. This involves inquiring about the number and ages of the children in an aspiring tenant's home.

- **Failing to make reasonable accommodations** – Landlords are required to offer reasonable accommodations for renters with disabilities, such as installing wheelchair ramps and permitting service animals. Failure to do so may constitute a violation of fair housing rules.

- **Source of income discrimination against tenants** – Landlords are not permitted to discriminate against tenants because of their source of income.

As a landlord, any of these actions will violate not just the federal Fair Housing Act, but also state and local regulations. As a result, it is critical that they understand how to avoid these violations, which we will go over in detail below.

Avoiding Fair Housing Law Violations

Fair housing rules violations can lead to hefty penalties, legal action, and reputational damage. So, here are some pointers to help you avoid breaking fair housing regulations as a landlord.

- *Understand applicable Fair Housing Laws* - Fair housing regulations differ by state and municipality, so it is critical to become acquainted with the precise rules that apply to your rental properties. These laws may encompass both the federal Fair Housing Act and state and municipal fair housing legislation. Discrimination on the basis of race, national origin, color, religion, familial status, sex, and disability are some frequent topics that are addressed by fair housing laws.
- *Use consistent screening criteria* - To guarantee that all potential tenants are treated equally, apply uniform screening criteria while analyzing applications. This includes confirming income, conducting credit checks, and validating employment, among other things. To avoid the impression of discrimination, ensure that these criteria are applied consistently to all candidates.
- *Avoid discrimination based on protected classes* - It is unlawful to treat prospective tenants differently on the basis of any of the protected qualities listed in fair housing regulations. This includes refusing to rent to someone based on their race or religion, as well as charging a higher rent to someone with a disability. It is also prohibited to make any statements or employ advertising that could be interpreted as discriminatory.
- *Create reasonable accommodations* - You are obligated to provide reasonable accommodations to a tenant with a disability whenever necessary, unless doing so would place excessive strain on you. Reasonable

accommodations may include building a wheelchair ramp or grab bars in the restroom.

- *Take caution when doing renovations and repairs* - If you are performing repairs or renovations to your rental premises, you must ensure that the alterations do not discriminate against tenants with disabilities. This could entail installing wheelchair ramps or ensuring that entrances and other places are large enough to accept mobility aids.

Finally, it's critical to understand the exceptions to the Fair Housing Law after gaining all the knowledge necessary to understand the exceptions to the law. We will discuss some of the Fair Housing Act's exceptions below.

Exemptions of Fair Housing Laws
As a landlord, you should be aware that there are several exceptions to Fair Housing Laws that may apply in certain situations. Landlords should be aware of the following typical exceptions to fair housing laws:

Owner-occupied buildings with four or fewer units: If you own a building with four or less units and live in one of them full-time, you may be exempt from fair housing regulations. However, it is crucial to note that this exclusion only applies to buildings with four or fewer units, and you may still be liable to fair housing regulations if you own a larger structure or do not live in one of the apartments as your primary place of residence.

Religious Organizations: Religious organizations, especially their schools and universities, are exempt from fair housing regulations. This means that these groups may be able to discriminate against people based on their faith when renting out housing units.

Single-family homes: If the owner owns no more than three single-family houses and does not rent them out through a real estate agent or broker, fair housing regulations do not apply. However, it is vital to remember that this provision does not apply to triplexes, duplexes, or other multi-family homes, even if the owner owns only one of them.

Leasing to a Family Member: Landlords are often not required to follow fair housing regulations when renting to a member of their own family. It should be noted that this exclusion solely pertains to the landlord's immediate family members; distinct individuals or members of their extended families are not covered.

Renting based on age: Fair housing rules may not expressly prohibit age discrimination, but some state and local legislation may provide additional protections for older people.

Landlord-Tenants Laws

Landlord-tenant rules differ from federal principles intended to safeguard renters. The Federal Fair Housing Act (FHA) outlaws housing discrimination. Unlike landlord-tenant regulations, which vary depending on where one may live, the FHA applies uniformly in all fifty states.

Another federal legislation that applies in all states is the Fair Credit Reporting Act, which specifies how a landlord can utilize your credit history for screening purposes. According to this rule, landlords must obtain the applicant's written consent before running a credit report, and they must notify you of the information contained in the report if it is the reason they are declining your credit application.

While each state has its own landlord-tenant legislation, there are certain similarities. Most states have laws concerning these subjects (but make sure to read the laws in your state to discover what applies where you live):

- *The right to quiet-enjoyment*: This law guarantees your right to live on the property without being disturbed. Essentially, as long as you reside on the property, you have the right to do so peacefully. This may be defined differently depending on where you live, but your state legislation may include anything about your right to privacy, which means your landlord cannot just show up unexpectedly (they must give advance warning) unless there is an emergency.
- *Right to a habitable condition*: The landlord is responsible for ensuring that the rental residence is safe and habitable. What this entails differs by state, so check your local laws. Essentially, it means that the rental residence must be safe and free of hazardous problems.
- *Laws for security deposits*: Many states have regula-tions governing security deposits. These laws may apply

to the full amount of any required security deposit. Many states do not have a maximum amount, so check the legislation where you live or want to move. State law may additionally specify how many days the landlord must return the security deposit at the end of the lease. If you hold all or a portion of the deposit, you may be obligated to furnish them with a written statement of any deductions made.

o *Laws for retaliatory conduct*: Several states have rules governing retaliatory behavior. This implies that tenants cannot be punished by a landlord for exercising their legal rights, such as complaining to a government agency about the safety or health conditions of a rental property, engaging in political or union activity, or bringing a complaint about housing discrimination.

Property Safety Regulations

A landlord's responsibility is to keep their leased property safe. Keeping your tenants for a longer amount of time requires that you provide a safe living environment. The simplest method to accomplish this is to maintain compliance with safety laws by conducting routine property inspections and scheduling walkthroughs to detect potential issues with the property. Preventive maintenance and early problem solving are the most effective approaches to avoid costly repairs.

In the following points, we will discuss what landlords may do to ensure that their property fulfills safety regulations.

- *Legal Requirements* - Every landlord must be aware of and follow local housing rules and regulations, which are intended to protect tenants' rights and safety. This involves following building laws, maintaining health and safety requirements, and ensuring the facility is habitable. Landlords must stay up to up-to-date on these rules, which could change and vary depending on area. Noncompliance can result in legal penalties and fines, as well as endangering tenants and jeopardizing the rental agreement's integrity.
- *Regular Maintenance and Inspections* - Regular maintenance and inspections are vital for detecting and adderssing any flaws before they become severe dangers. This includes inspecting structural integrity, electrical systems, plumbing, and appliances to ensure they are in working order. In addition to extending the life of the property and preventing accidents and injuries, routine maintenance can also save money over time by preventing expensive emergency repairs. It indicates a landlord's dedication to maintaining a secure and cozy living space.
- *Fire Safety Standards* - Fire safety is critical in any dwelling. Landlords are responsible for installing fire extinguishers, smoke detectors, and, if necessary, fire sprinkler systems. It's also critical to have clear escape routes that are never blocked. Regular checks should be performed to verify that all fire safety equipment is in excellent working order. Educating tenants about fire

safety protocols and how to utilize fire safety equipment can help to improve safety measures.

- *Health and Environmental Standards* - This includes keeping the rental home free of health dangers such mold, asbestos, lead paint, and bugs. Proper ventilation, safe drinking water, and effective waste disposal systems are all essential for sustaining a healthy living environment. Compliance with environmental regulations promotes tenant well-being while also contributing to the larger goal of environmental sustainability. Regularly addressing these concerns can help to avoid long-term health hazards and legal complications.

- *Tenant Safety Education* - Educating renters on safety precautions, emergency procedures, and their obligetions can greatly improve overall safety. This may include instructions on how to operate appliances properly, what to do in the event of a gas leak, fire evacuation routes, and how to report maintenance issues. Giving tenants this knowledge enables them to respond appropriately and quickly in potentially hazardous situations, lowering the chance of accidents.

- *Documentation and Certification Compliance* – Landlords should maintain detailed records of all maintenance work, safety inspections, and adherence to local requirements. This includes certifications for gas safety, electrical safety, and energy efficiency, among other things. Proper paperwork is not only a legal obligation, but it also acts as proof of the landlord's commitment to upholding the property's safety standards. In the event of a disagreement or an inspection, well-kept records can serve as evidence of compliance and responsible management.

Why are Safety Regulations Important?

Landlords should ensure that their rental properties fulfill safety requirements for a variety of reasons, all of which contribute to a more secure, safer, and legally compliant rental business. Here's why landlords should prioritize property safety.

Legal compliance and liability reduction: In most areas, meeting safety requirements is required by law. It is the landlord's responsibility to give occupants a safe and livable space. Breaking these guidelines can result in legal consequences such as fines and litigation. By adhering to safety requirements, landlords can reduce their liability and protect themselves from litigation stemming from negligence or safety violations.

Tenants safety and well-being: The most important reason for meeting safety regulations is to safeguard the physical safety and well-being of renters. A safe facility reduces the chance of injuries, accidents, and health problems, which are critical to renters' quality of life. Landlords have an ethical and moral obligation to guarantee that their property poses no risks to individuals who live there.

Property preservation: Consistent maintenance and conformity to safety regulations aid in maintaining the property's condition and worth. If left untreated, issues such as water leaks, electrical difficulties, or structural deficiencies can cause serious harm. Landlords who keep their properties in good shape might avoid costly repairs in the future and ensure that the property retains, or even enhances, its value with time.

Tenant satisfactions and retention: Tenants are more inclined to renew their rents in places that make them feel protected and respected. Landlords help to create a favorable living environment by ensuring a property satisfies safety regulations, which increases tenant happiness and loyalty. Tenants who are satisfied are more likely to take better care of the property, which reduces wear and tear and maintenance costs.

Insurance compliance: Insurance companies frequently demand homes to meet particular safety standards in order to provide coverage. Failure to meet these standards may result in the denial of insurance claims or possibly the cancellation of the policy. Ensuring a property fulfills safety standards allows landlords to keep their insurance coverage, which provides financial protection against potential losses or liability claims.

Reputation and Marketability: A well-kept, safe property appeals to prospective tenants and might earn higher rents. Landlords that are known for upholding strong safety standards improve their reputation in the rental market. This reputation can lead to faster tenant turnover, increased demand for their property, and possibly better rental income.

Ensuring that your rental property complies with safety regulations is not only about checking boxes; it's also about providing your tenants with a great living environment, peace of mind, and legal compliance. If this seems too much, think about working with a professional in property management.

Benefits of Being a Landlord

One of the best ways to increase wealth and create passive income is to invest in rental property and become a landlord. Although it requires commitment and time, being a landlord offers numerous advantages, making it a worthwhile endeavor. Being a landlord has a number of benefits, some of which are listed here.

Steady passive stream of income: Being able to earn a consistent income is one of the most major advantages of being a landlord. Renting out a property allows you to collect monthly rent payments that cover your mortgage, insurance, property taxes, and other expenditures. Rental income is frequently more stable than other sources of income, making it a safe and profitable investment. Being a landlord often generates passive income. This means you don't have to work hard to earn it. This allows you to reap the benefits of rental income while also having time to pursue other interests, such as your profession or hobbies.

Property appreciation value: Ownership of a rental property can also result in long-term property value appreciation. Your investment will yield a substantial return as the property's value rises over time (if such property is in the right area). In addition, tax benefits including depreciation and deductions for property taxes and mortgage interest are available to property owners.

Flexibility: Owning rental property provides a lot of flexibility. For example, you can pick when to rent the home, how long the contract will last, and what the rental rate will be. You can also manage the property yourself or engage a property management company to handle responsibilities like tenant screening, rent collecting, and maintenance.

Tax Benefits: The United States tax code has provisions that favor those who rent out residential units. One of the benefits of being a landlord is the option to deduct a wide range of expenses if their rental revenue results in a net loss. This may appear to be a negative, but you can offset this net loss with other sources of money, such as your wage income from employment.

- *Mortgage interest*: This is frequently the largest tax deduction available to landlords. This includes payments for the interest on a mortgage used to purchase or improve rental property.
- *Depreciation*: Over a period of twenty-seven and a half years, residential landlords are able to deduct from their taxes the purchase price of the rental property.
- *Repairs*: For the tax year in which they paid for the repairs, landlords are able to deduct repairs made to the rental property as a result of their obligations, such as painting, plumbing, etc.

- *Travel*: Landlords may deduct travel expenditures connected to their landlord responsibilities. Maintain proper records as the Internal Revenue Service (IRS) examines these deductions.
- *Home office*: If they meet the conditions, landlords are able to deduct the costs associated with running a home office.

Financial security: As a landlord, investing in rental properties provides financial security and stability. Your sense of financial security will increase when your rental income is consistent. This will provide you a sense of security and peace of mind, especially in these difficult economic times.

CHAPTER TWO
GETTING STARTED IN PROPERTY MANAGEMENT

Property management involves more than just keeping a property in good condition; it also includes effectively managing its finances. Effective financial management is essential for successful property management, particularly in the field of house ownership. The ability to manage finances and budgets effectively has a direct impact on the profitability and long-term viability of any property venture. A well-managed financial plan ensures that properties not only retain their value, but also generate satisfactory returns. It includes a wide range of vital duties, including accurate budget planning and spending tracking, as well as strategic income optimization.

It aids in the mitigation of property management risks such as unanticipated maintenance expenses and fluctuating occupancy rates. Ultimately, successful financial management is about more than just maintaining assets; it's about enhancing their value.

Start off with a Solid Budget

Developing a solid budget is an important step in commercial property management that ensures financial stability and success. The approach starts with a thorough review of previous financial performance. This entails evaluating past years' income and expenses to identify trends and anomalies. From there, accurately projecting future income is critical. This includes calculating rental income using current leases and market trends, as well as taking into account potential vacancies and rate of turnover.

The next action is to list all anticipated costs. In commercial property management, they might include everything from routine maintenance and repairs to property taxes, insurance, and management fees. It is critical to set aside funds for unforeseen repairs or emergencies, as they can have a big influence on the budget. The best budgeting methods include examining and revising the budget on a regular basis. Market conditions and property requirements can vary; therefore, flexibility and adaptation are vital. Regular evaluations enable adjustments to be made in reaction to these developments, ensuring the budget's accuracy and effectiveness.

Expense Management: keeping costs in check

Property management relies heavily on effectively managing and minimizing expenses. Maintenance and repair charges are one of the most common expenses in this field. Regular maintenance is necessary for property care, but it must be balanced against cost efficiency. Implementing a preventative maintenance program will help you avoid larger, more expensive issues in the future. Property management costs are another big expense that should be reviewed on a regular basis to verify that they are reasonable for the service delivered.

Utility expenditures can be a significant expense, particularly in larger properties. Implementing energy-efficient solutions and encouraging renters to save energy can result in significant savings. Furthermore, insurance and property taxes are recurrent expenses that must be properly monitored. Shopping around for competitive insurance rates, as well as appealing property tax assessments where appropriate, can help to decrease these expenditures.

Renovation management requires careful planning and budgeting to minimize overspending. Prioritizing renovations that raise property value or save long-term maintenance costs may be more financially advantageous. Property managers can greatly enhance their financial performance by regularly monitoring these typical expenses and identifying strategies to optimize them.

Income Optimization Strategies

Successful property management revolves around maximizing rental income. Setting competitive rent rates is critical; this includes analyzing local market trends to make sure your rates are consistent with similar rental properties in the region. It is critical to find a balance between competitive pricing and profit maximization, taking into account aspects such as amenities, property location, and the current real estate market.

Aside from rental income, pursuing alternative revenue streams can greatly increase overall earnings. This could involve charging an additional cost for luxury services such as storage, parking, or high-speed internet. Vending machines and coin-operated laundry facilities can also provide additional revenue when implemented appropriately.

Rental income is directly impacted by tenant retention and marketing strategies that work. High tenant turnover might result in lost revenue and higher costs. As a result, maintaining positive tenant relationships, responding quickly to repair and maintenance issues, and keeping the property in good condition are critical for tenant retention.

Finally, renovation management is vital for maximizing profits. Thoughtful upgrades can justify rent increases, improve property appeal, and attract higher-paying tenants. Focusing on upgrades that tenants value the most, such as new kitchens or bathrooms, might result in a better return on investment (ROI). These strategies enable property managers to properly optimize their income and ensure the profitability of their properties.

Effectively Using Financial Management Tool

In the realm of property management, utilizing technology via financial management tools and software is critical for efficiency and accuracy. These solutions range from complete property management software that incorporates financial tracking with other property management activities to specialized accounting software designed specifically for property management.

One of the most significant advantages of employing these technologies is their ability to automate normal financial processes such as rent collection, spending tracking, and financial reporting. This automation saves time while also reducing the possibility of human error. Furthermore, many of these software solutions include real-time financial data analysis, allowing property managers direct insight into their properties' financial performance.

Another key benefit is the ease of budgeting and forecasting. Advanced software can assist property managers in forecasting future income and expenses based on existing data, allowing them to make more informed financial decisions. These tools are invaluable for property sourcers because they allow them to rapidly and precisely examine the financial sustainability of possible properties.

Overall, the use of financial management software and tools streamlines financial processes in property management, offering a clear, structured perspective of financial health and assisting with strategic decision-making.

Navigating Taxation

Taxation and compliance are two complex but essential components of property management. The numerous tax laws that property managers have to deal with can differ greatly based on the property's location and kind. Understanding these tax requirements is critical for avoiding penalties and maximizing tax benefits.

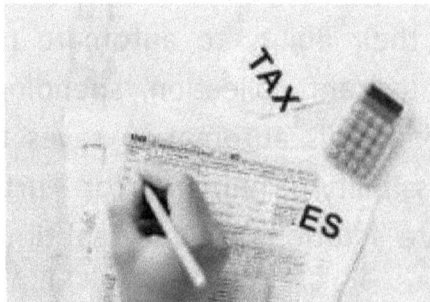

Property tax is one important area where managers need to stay current on local tax rates and assessment procedures. Property tax assessments that are appealed in certain circumstances may save a lot of money. Another crucial issue is income tax on rental revenue, where understanding permitted deductions can have a major impact on net income from the property.

Financial regulation compliance is equally as important as taxation. This involves following fair housing regulations, keeping adequate financial records, and ensuring that all financial transactions are compliant with local and federal laws. Failure to comply might result in legal consequences and financial penalties.

Staying up to date on the newest tax rules and regulations is critical for property sourcing and management. Using the experience of tax professionals and legal consultants, as well as being up to date on legislative changes, can help you negotiate these complexities more successfully. Ensuring compliance helps the business stay out of legal hot water and enhances its overall financial stability and reputation.

Setting Realistic Goals

When opting to become a landlord and purchase property for buy-to-let purposes, it is important to have a clear under-standing of your investing objectives. What exactly do you aim to achieve? Regarding the purchase of a buy-to-let property. This could come from either:

- A capital profit target (due to rising property prices)
- An income goal for the property based on monthly payments from a tenant.
- A combination of the aforementioned.

Rental incomes are usually quite constant, ranging between 0% and 20%. A portion of your preparatory effort will involve locating properties that will be simple to rent; doing so will help to guarantee that there are fewer void periods between rentals. Property prices are more variable, but unless you want to make immediate short-term gains, determining when to buy will not be too difficult. Even in cases where situations temporarily worsen, social and economic changes indicate that the long-term trend should be upward.

Investment Mentality - various people have various attitudes toward risk and investment; your approach or mindset to making money from property investment should account for swings in both local and national housing markets. Local markets frequently behave differently than national markets; therefore, knowing your local area or conducting a thorough analysis of the wants and needs in your chosen location is critical. Paying attention to local news, which details changes in local requirements, can also pay off. As a Buy to Let investor, you should strive to make medium to long-term investments, which will help smooth out any short-term (downward) property market swings.

Short-term property price purchases are typically reserved for speculators, and unless you have a solid understanding of the market, you could lose a lot of money. You should aim for a combination of rental income and capital appreciation. Always seek professional counsel before making a purchase, and strive to find value in whatever property you acquire. Local professionals can be a wonderful source of free information, alerting you to buy-to-let property discounts while also assisting you in achieving your long-term goals. Don't make the common error of believing that you always know best; instead, be willing to listen and receive counsel. Finally, the important success elements (whether income or profit-based) will be:

- o Minimizing rental voids - This is a buy-to-let landlord's worst nightmare; even short periods of empty property can have a negative impact on your estimates.
- o Effectively controlling your cost structure to maximize long-term rental returns can be accomplished by paying close attention to the property you purchase and matching it as closely as possible to local market needs.

Achievable Investment Goals - To financially quantify and define your goals, you must do a thorough study of your spending and consider changes in financial variables. Be realistic, try to look at things from a worst-case scenario perspective, and assume, as most people do, that property values will rise, mortgage rates will remain stable, and you will always be able to find a suitable tenant, thus avoiding the rental avoidances that everyone else seems to experience. Many people could save thousands of pounds if they took the time to do these calculations.

Buy-to-let investing is not for everyone, and the "buy-to-let journey" should begin with these calculations rather than attempting to find a property. Make sure your goals are attainable, and think about how much time you will need to devote to this endeavor. Logistics are also crucial; a house in Scotland may be tough to manage if you reside in Devon. You might need to use a local letting agent's services.

Objective Goal Setting - Your primary motivation for entering the buy-to-let market is to create investments that will eventually improve your financial status or give you long-term financial stability. Remember this at all times: you must keep emotion out of your decisions. Purchasing property is simply another type of objective investment, but because tenants are involved, there's a human component to the scenario. Most people consider dealing with tenants to be the most challenging component of property management, and some-times unpleasant decisions must be made.

If you have trouble interacting with people in person when they occasionally have financial issues or want to voice a complaint about the rental property, you might be better off hiring a property expert, like a letting agent, to handle these negotiations on your behalf. While treating tenants fairly and equally is important, it's definitely best to avoid being too friendly. Be professional in your transactions so that everyone understands where they stand.

Before you begin, calculate how much money you will need to invest, how much you want to make from the sale of the property, and all of the deductions that will be required along the route. Knowing your starting and finishing points, as well as any points in between, will allow you to better track your progress. Remember the acronym S.M.A.R.T. This stands for "Specific, Measurable, Accurate, Realistic, and Timely." It's incredible how many people jump into an investing concept without paying close attention to what they're doing.

Capital Profit - The primary purpose of capital profit is to profit from increases in property value. Taking this approach implies that you believe the price of the property will increase over the time frame you have set. You will normally be required to put down a deposit to acquire the home, with the remainder of the purchase price supported by a buy-to-let mortgage. The mortgage payments are made by renting out the house to a tenant. This investing aim is based on the gearing principle.

The word "capital gearing," which originates from Britain, describes how much debt a business has in comparison to its equity. In the US, capital gearing, also known as "financial leverage" - is the smart use of borrowed funds to invest in assets. The idea is for the return on such assets to be greater than the cost of borrowing capital.

Logic dictates that the more properties you own, the higher your capital gearing (profit). Of course, property prices might fall and interest rates can rise, which are some of the hazards associated with this sort of investment. By properly picking your property, you can help maximize your profits. House prices are generally expected to rise in value over time due to inflation.

Rental Income - The main goal is to choose a rent that will not only pay your monthly mortgage and all expenses, but will also provide you with a residual income. Once the mortgage is paid off, you can sell the house for a profit or keep it and live on the income. You need to consider this throughout the planning stage because it is quite improbable that one property will be enough to live off of. When it comes to handling the rental money from the property, there are two main options. One way is to use the extra funds to pay off the mortgage as soon as possible, and your personal situation and current interest rates will guide your decision.

Once the mortgage is paid off, you will own the asset altogether, and the monthly rental will become part of your earnings. Of course, you may decide to just spend the extra money you receive each month on rent. If you want to do this, you should generally look for a home with a greater rental yield (such as student or HMO housing). These types of properties do not typically provide such high capital growth.

Planning Considerations - Before approaching a mortgage lender to obtain a loan, you must first choose your investment goal(s). You should consider the following points.

- Consider how many houses you plan to buy. If you intend to buy more than one, you must ensure that your mortgage lender will not impose any restrictions on the size of your portfolio or the overall value of the property you're buying. Lenders are now extremely cautious due to the situation in the industry.
- Consider what type of renter you want to attract. Some lenders may not want to lend on houses that will be rented to students, DSS, local governments, or housing organizations. The type of tenant may be taken into account when the lender reviews your application.
- Consider the type of property you want to buy; while most will be private dwelling houses, others will be HMOs, ex-council housing, or even flats. Many lenders may be hesitant to take on these types of risks due to additional regulatory restrictions.
- Consider the amount of money you can afford to invest. The lender will normally ask you to pay a deposit, which might now be a significant fraction of the required loan amount.

Landlord Rental Terms

Short-Term Rentals

Short-term rentals, as the name implies, are residences that are rented out for a short period of time, often a few days to a few weeks. These rentals have grown in prominence in recent years, thanks in part to platforms that allow for such arrangements. Some classic examples include holiday rentals, when guests book residences for vacation stays; Airbnb, a platform that connects homeowners with travelers looking for unique accommodation experiences; and weekend rents, which are frequently used by those looking for a quick break or temporary housing option.

Advantages of Short-term Rentals

- *Potential for greater Rental Income*: Unlike long-term leases, which frequently have fixed rates for longer periods of time, short-term rentals allow landlords to charge a premium, particularly during special events or peak seasons, potentially contributing to a greater total income.
- *Flexibility in Property Usage*: As tenants come and go, you have additional opportunity to access and use the property for personal purposes or in between bookings.
- *Easier to Keep Up with Repairs*: Because of the regular turnovers, it is typically easier to notice and address maintenance issues quickly, ensuring that the property remains in good shape.
- *Opportunity for frequent price adjustments*: The short-term market's dynamic nature allows you to modify prices often in response to factors such as demand, local events, or seasonality, maximizing income potential.

Disadvantages of Short-term Rentals

- *More Maintenance and Cleaning Responsibilities*: While it might be profitable, managing frequent departures and arrivals can be taxing. This frequently entails extra cleaning, administration, and management.

- *Seasonal Income Fluctuations*: Unlike long-term leases, which are predictable, short-term rentals may produce large returns during peak season but be quiet during off-peak seasons, resulting in irregular revenue streams.
- *High Operating Costs*: Frequent tenant turnover raises expenditures, ranging from cleaning fees to electricity and operating charges such as towels, linens, and toilet paper.
- *Property-Selective*: Not every property is suitable for a constant turnover of tenants. The short-term rental model's suitability can be determined by factors such as property type, geography, and even municipal restrictions.

Long-Term Rentals

Long-term rentals are residences that are rented out for an extended period of time, typically ranging from several months to one year. This conventional approach to home rental continues to be a staple of the rental industry. The most frequent types are standard leases, which specify terms and conditions for durations often lasting a year, and yearly contracts, which bind both tenants and landlords to a fixed agreement that lasts 12 months.

Advantages of Long-term Rentals

- *Monthly cash*: With a longer-term tenant, landlords may expect a constant and predictable cash stream each month.
- *Reduced Tenant Turnovers*: When tenants live in a property for longer stretches of time, there's less need for ongoing tenant onboarding, screening, and advertising.
- *Less Daily Management Required*: There is a significant reduction in daily management when compared to short-term rentals, which undergo a constant cycle of check-ins and check-outs.
- *Easier Finance and Budget Forecast*: Budgeting and financial forecasting are made easier by the steadiness of long-term leases, which provide constant earnings and predictable expenses.

Disadvantage of Short-term Rentals

- *Properties Are More Vulnerable to Damage*: While it's not a guarantee, extended stays may cause more deterioration, particularly if tenants eventually grow accustomed to not caring for the house.
- *Diminished Profit Margins*: Although revenue remains consistent, long-term rentals may not have the same premium pricing options as short-term leases, particularly during times of high demand.
- *Less Freedom to Enter the Property*: Landlords may find it difficult to enter their properties whenever they choose, for inspections or personal usage, as a result of renters signing longer leases.

- *Rent increases may be constrained*: Landlords may find themselves unable to modify rent costs in reaction to market shifts because they are bound by extended lease periods and, in some cases, municipal legislation.

Key Factors in Decision Making

When deciding between short-term and long-term leases, several key issues emerge. These considerations go beyond prospective revenues and include the nature of the property, your personal preferences, and the larger area in which you operate. Here's a close look:

Local market condition

- o *Location's Tourism Appeal*: Short-term rentals are naturally drawn to properties situated in popular tourist areas. This is because high-tourism areas frequently see increases in demand, particularly during peak seasons or events.
- o *Demand and Supply in Long-Term Housing*: On the other hand, if your property has a growing local population and a significant shortfall in long-term housing options, a long-term rental may be more profitable and reliable.

Personal financial goals

- o *Need for Stable Income*: If your primary goal is to ensure a consistent monthly income without the ups and downs of seasonal fluctuations, long-term rentals may be more appealing to you.

- *Prospective Income Maximization*: On the other hand, short-term rentals provide you the freedom to change rates and maybe make more money if you're trying to take advantage of busy times and don't mind fluctuations.

Management Preferences
- *Willingness to Regularly Manage Property*: Are you ready for routine check-ins and check-outs, tenant turnovers, and other details associated with short-term rentals? If so, this could be the right path for you.
- *Desire for a hands-off approach*: Long-term rentals may be more appealing if you want to be less involved in day-to-day operations and have fewer tenant interactions.

Property Characteristics
- Is the property better suited for vacationers or long-term residents? Think about your property's design, features, and location. A house near tourist attractions may be ideal for vacation rentals, whilst a suburban family home may appeal to long-term tenants.

Mitigating Risks

Being a landlord has risks, whether you pick short-term or long-term rentals. From potential property damage to legal difficulties, it is critical to be proactive in mitigating these risks. The following are critical tactics to assist you handle challenges in any rental terms:

Screening Tenants/Guests Properly

- o *Diligence is Vital*: Before concluding a rental agreement, it is critical to vet potential renters or guests. Long-term tenants may be required to provide references, credit checks, and rental histories. For short-term guests, examining profiles, reviews, and feedback on platforms such as Airbnb can provide useful information.

Having Comprehensive Insurance Covering

- o *Tailored Protection*: Make sure your insurance policy is specifically geared to your type of rental. While regular homes insurance may suffice for long-term rentals, short-term rentals may necessitate additional coverage, particularly if you host visitors frequently.

Comprehension and Compliance with Local Regulation

- o *Stay Current*: Rental restrictions vary greatly depending on area and can change over time. Make it a priority to stay current on local laws, zoning rules, and any licensing requirements that may apply to your rental plan.

Establishing Clear House Rules and Rental Agreements

- o *Establish Expectations*: Whether it's a formal lease agreement for a long-term tenant or house rules for a weekend visitor, clarity is key. To avoid misunderstandings and disagreements, fully outline terms such as payment timelines and behavioral expectations.

<u>Considering Property Management Service</u>

o *Professional Support*: If the thought of overseeing renters, taking care of maintenance, or answering reservations seems overwhelming, you might want to think about working with a property management company. They can relieve a lot of the manual labor, improve the visitor or renter experience, and simplify operations, all of which can provide you with peace of mind.

Both rental systems have advantages and disadvantages, ranging from the potential profitability of short-term rentals during peak seasons to the consistent income stream and simplicity of maintenance provided by long-term leases.

As a landlord, you must realize that there is no one-size-fits-all solution. Your optimum choice is determined by a variety of factors, including financial goals, property attributes, and personal management preferences. The local market conditions, regulatory framework, and core of what you aim to achieve with your property are all important factors in this decision-making process.

Rental Market Analysis

Rental market analysis (RMA) is critical for landlords, investors, and property managers across all real estate markets. It makes understanding the rental market easier and encourages educated decision-making by removing guesswork.

Imagine owning a crystal ball that could tell you anything you wanted to know about the rental market right now, including how to set competitive rentals, spot profitable investments, and create property offers that would entice buyers. That's what a complete RMA provides.

RMA delves deeply into the mechanics of demand and supply, rental pricing points, and the numerous variables that influence rental rates and property values. It's not just about keeping your home occupied; it's also about maximizing its earning potential and ensuring long-term value.

What is Rental Market Analysis?
Rental market analysis (RMA) is a thorough evaluation used by real estate brokers, investors, landlords, and property managers to assess the present health of the rental market, identify trends, and make sound decisions about property investment and management.

This analysis aids in your comprehension of the dynamics of supply and demand for rental properties within a certain market or region, as well as the evaluation of rental price points and the variables affecting both rental rates and property prices. It is necessary for maximizing rental income, increasing property value, and planning developments or future investments. Below is a step by step guide to conducting an analysis on the local rental market.

Step One: Identifying Comparable Properties
The first stage in an RMA is to identify properties that are comparable to the subject property in terms of size, location,

and attributes. These "comps," or comparable properties, provide a standard by which to measure the market worth of the underlying property. Looking at previously rented properties in close proximity guarantees that the data is relevant and gives insight into what potential renters are willing to pay for comparable houses.

Step Two: Analyzing Rental Rates and Analyzing Local Market
Once rental comparables have been discovered, the next step is to assess the local market's demand and current rental rates. This research entails looking at comparable property occupancy rates, rental turnover rates, and any seasonal swings in rental demand. Understanding these components allows you to price the property competitively, ensuring that it reflects the current market situation and tenants' expectations.

Step Three: Evaluating property condition, location and amenities
The rental value of a property is heavily influenced by its location, condition, and amenities. Properties in desirable locations, in outstanding condition, and with sought-after amenities can command higher rental rates. This process entails a detailed evaluation of the subject property in comparison to the competitors, taking into account any distinguishing qualities or potential downsides.

Step Four: Understanding the impact of Demographic and Economic trends
The final step in completing an RMA is to evaluate the larger demographic and economic trends affecting the rental

market. Economic indicators such as employment, income, and population growth can have a substantial impact on rental demand and pricing. Furthermore, demographic factors, such as the tastes of different age groups or the arrival of new people in a neighborhood, might alter the types of homes in demand.

Conducting a thorough rental market analysis necessitates research and an awareness of the micro and macroeconomic aspects that drive the rental market. Following these steps will provide landlords and investors with significant market knowledge, allowing them to make sound decisions that enhance their investment potential. This strategic strategy ensures that the property remains competitive in the current market while also ensuring its long-term viability as a successful rental investment.

Analyzing Rental Market Trends and Property Rates
Navigating the ever-changing rental market situation necessitates a thorough awareness of property prices and general market trends. This knowledge is critical for landlords and investors looking to optimize their rental strategy and keep their properties competitive and profitable.

Below, we cover efficient strategies for accessing and evaluating critical data on housing market and rental rates changes, emphasize the need to remain on top of these developments, and look at how technology and internet resources may be valuable partners in monitoring market dynamics.

Accessing and interpreting data on rental rates and market trends

Finding the right places to look is the first step in comprehending rental prices, property values, and market trends. Various web platforms, real estate databases, and property management software provide detailed information on rental pricing, occupancy rates, and market variations.

Local property listings, websites for rental properties, and publications on real estate market analysis are important sources of property data. Landlords and investors can use this data to analyze average rental rates for similar properties in particular areas, identify trends in the demand for rentals, and see how outside variables affect the behavior of the rental property market.

It's crucial to take the surrounding circumstances—such as the local economy, changing demographics, and any modifications to real estate laws—into account while analyzing this data. In addition to helping forecast future trends, analyzing these variables in conjunction with rental rate data offers a more in-depth understanding of the particular real estate market.

Importance of Staying Up-to-date with Market Trends

Keeping up with the newest market developments is critical for maintaining a competitive advantage. Demand and rental pricing can be greatly impacted by market trends, which can also have an impact on the speed at which a property gets leased out and how profitable it is.

For example, an increase in demand within a specific location or demographic may justify a rental price hike, whereas a saturated market may necessitate adjustments to remain competitive. By keeping a regular eye on these patterns, rental price tactics can be adjusted to maximize revenue and occupancy while also taking into account the state of the market.

Leveraging online resources and technology

Technology is essential for streamlining the dynamics of the rental market tracking process. Real-time data and predicted insights into market patterns can be found on the internet through resources including property management software, rental market analysis tools, and real estate analytics platforms.

Quick and effective data-driven decision making is made possible for landlords and investors by features like automated comp analysis, market reports, and rental price estimators. Social media and real estate-related internet forums can also be helpful resources, providing first hand views of market circumstances as well as networking opportunities with other real estate professionals.

Furthermore, using property management solutions that include market analysis functions can help streamline operations and guarantee rental costs are always competitive with current market rates.

This analysis not only sheds light on the current status of the market, but also aids in forecasting future trends, ensuring

that rental policies stay responsive and matched with changing market conditions.

CHAPTER THREE

FINDING AND ASSESSING RENT PROPERTY

Finding the ideal rental property can seem like a difficult task. It might be challenging to know where to begin with so many alternatives available. Of course, securing a fantastic investment requires more than just a keen eye; it also requires excellent detective abilities and contacts with people in the know. However, purchasing a rental property doesn't have to be challenging. In fact, knowing what you're searching for makes it a lot easier the next time around. Of course, you'll want to familiarize yourself with the processes beforehand, and having connections in the field can facilitate this. However, there are plenty of things you can do on your own to find suitable homes and make sure the one you buy turns out to be a wise investment.

Identifying Potential Investment Properties

First and foremost, it's critical to begin by considering your strategic objectives. Selecting success with rental property is more than just selecting a rental and hoping for the best; it is also important to ensure that the property you invest in meets your criteria. Hence, start by taking the time to establish your big goals. What level of cash flow are you hoping to achieve? After costs and taxes, how much profit would you like to make? Are you seeking appreciation, cash flow, or both kinds of returns? This will ultimately help you make an informed decision about which property to invest in as well as which market to invest in.

Which kind of property is best for investing? That will depend on your objectives, tastes, and financial situation. Are you searching for a consistent, dependable source of income or a high-yield, high-risk opportunity? It is advisable to take into account the kind of rental property that is most in demand in the area where you intend to make an investment. Which types of properties are more in demand: holiday rentals, multi-unit buildings, or single-family homes? Before making a decision, find out what people actually need.

You may also think about the distinctions between purchasing a newly built property and an existing one. Newly built homes typically have competitive pricing, modern facilities, and customizable options. But there may be dangers, such as higher expenses, longer completion times, and the unpredictability of a freshly established neighborhood. The benefits of existing properties include access, convenience, and well-established amenities; the drawbacks could be exorbitant property prices or the need for expensive maintenance for older properties.

Ultimately, the ideal rental is one that fits your needs, budget, and experience.

Consider the Location
In the world of property management, location is everything. Many investors search emerging markets—areas that are expanding now and are predicted to do so in the future—for rental properties. Look for places where there is a robust labor market and a growing population. There is an increase in both jobs and population in some places in the Sun Belt and South. Try to locate properties in places where the annual rent increase and property appreciation have been steady over the past few years. Remarkable surroundings can attract long-term tenants of high caliber. The year-round attraction of strong schools, institutions, and job opportunities is likely to draw in both working adults and students.

Another benefit is that public transportation is easily accessible. Renters enjoy the ease with which they may travel to work, school, or other important locations without using a car when they live in a neighborhood. Tenants benefit from this by saving time and money and having an easier time getting around the neighborhood. Long-term strategic investment opportunities might also arise from purchasing rental properties near public transportation. In general, property values near frequent public transportation tend to appreciate more.

Consider Neighborhood Safety and Amenities
It's crucial to consider factors other than the house itself when trying to purchase a rental property. Think about the surroundings as well. For many tenants, having quick access to shopping outlets and various businesses is a big plus. Features like a playground, park, or pool are excellent additions that raise the location's overall appeal and have an impact on rental demand. For instance, young, working families with children will find great appeal in a house located in a neighborhood with lots of green space and a playground.

The neighborhood's safety and security are also quite important. Investigate the local crime rate, take some time to study it, and get further information by talking to locals or the authorities. Getting a first-hand look at the community can also be accomplished by paying a visit. When doing a neighborhood survey, keep an eye out for some of these possible warning signs:

- Inadequate street lighting
- Very few children play outside.
- Heavy police presence
- Abandoned stores
- Unkempt parks
- Properties in poor condition (broken windows, over-grown yards, etc.)

Consider the State of the Property

There are properties in every condition, from recently built and ready to move into to fixer-uppers. Some investors find fixer-uppers appealing. They are, however, not for the faint-hearted!

A fixer-upper is a house in poor condition that someone purchases with the goal of working on it, renovating it, and elevating its worth.

It may not be financially viable or realistic unless you have the necessary resources and experience. This is due to the possibility that you will also need to devote a significant quantity of time or energy to the project. Make sure it will be financially feasible as well. To obtain a more accurate estimate of the time and cost of repairs, try to have the property professionally inspected. Next, establish realistic forecasts to see if your anticipated return on investment (ROI) is worth it.

A well-maintained property will save you money on upkeep and repairs and is more likely to draw in decent tenants. Do a comprehensive inspection of the entire property before purchasing any form of real estate. Keep an eye out for indications of possible remodeling projects, plumbing or electrical problems, and structural damage. Seek inspectors' advice, decide which repairs are best left to outside contractors, and obtain quotes for large-scale repairs. Determine how long repairs would take; if they are going to take a while, it may not be worthwhile. You will have to wait a lot longer to start making money from a property that will be vacant for an extended length of time. Before investing in a fixer-upper, you should ensure that you have sufficient funds or financing, to cover the repairs.

Assess the Market Conditions

Understanding the local real estate market is essential before making an investment because real estate trends are subject to change. Depending on the property and the state of the market, high net worth investors may decide to invest in pricey markets in order to receive greater rentals and, in certain situations, higher long-term appreciation. However, if you're just getting started with investing, you might want to think about taking a look at less expensive places to see what's available. Your investment should bring in enough money each month to pay for all of your expenses and turn a profit. For many investors, determining a market in which the property is expected to appreciate over time is another crucial factor.

Research and remain current with trends on:

- Rental prices, vacancy rates, local property values, and trends in demand for rentals
- Local economic indicators include population growth and job diversity, among others.
- The potential for economic growth in the neighborhood, the improvements to the infrastructure, and any forthcoming initiatives that might have a beneficial effect on the rental market

Consider Property Taxes

Different locations have different property taxes. While paying high property taxes can reduce your rental income, they are not always a bad thing. Certain communities or neighborhoods that have higher housing demand may have high property taxes. The value of a property is taken into account while calculating property taxes. That covers the surrounding terrain as well as any extra buildings. A property may have a greater property tax than its next-door neighbor if it has a bigger home, more land area, or other desirable attributes.

Weigh up Profit Potential and Cash Flow

Make sure to assess the investment's possible cash flow as well. A solid financial plan is crucial, as is a safety net for unforeseen costs or vacant periods. Your rental revenue should cover not just your mortgage payments, but also other expenses like property taxes, insurance, maintenance charges, and property management fees. Analyze comparable rental prices in the area to determine the property's rental potential. Assessing comparable properties aids in estimating your prospective rental revenue. Take into account the local occupancy rate as well as the typical length of time it takes to find tenants.

Before investing in a property, you should run the numbers to check if the predicted returns are in line with your goals. One reliable measure of your return on investment (ROI) is cash-on-cash returns. It is the proportion of the initial cash investment to the cash flow that the investment generates. In order to get a favorable cash-on-cash return, it is advisable to seek out properties with higher potential rental revenue. Here are your profit and spending projections:

- The expected rise in long-term appreciation
- Expected cash flow from rental income
- Tax benefits and depreciation

Keep an Eye on Future Development
Look into any upcoming or current changes that might affect the property's worth or rental prospects. In a few years, the broad, open green space behind a residential building might turn into a loud factory complex, which would lower its value. Similarly, a new high-rise can block your condo's expansive views of the seashore. Look into the intended use of the surroundings near the investment property.

However, favorable developments in the future can raise the value and desirability of a property. This covers new transportation links, business developments, and infrastructural initiatives. Long-term, favorable developments might increase rental demand and property values, increasing the appeal of your investment.

Evaluating Property Value and Rental Potential

Research is the most important thing you should do. When thinking about investing in rental properties, you can apply common sense. Rental income from a single-family home will be on the upper side. The next-highest monthly rent is for a side-by-side. Duplexes are the next most profitable type of real estate. Properties with three or four units in a single, two-story building will have the lowest monthly rent.

Estimate Rental Income

The next thing you need to do is calculate the possible rent amount. You can take your time browsing through real estate websites to find the market pricing for rent. It is important to ensure that the properties you are considering are physically close to your own, as rental prices might differ greatly across different areas. Additionally, you should confirm that the rental homes you are evaluating are situated in similar neighborhoods.

You'll discover when you compile your rental data that comparable properties have a wide variety of rents. The properties at the lowest end are probably subpar apartments that require a lot of maintenance. The apartments with lots of amenities and are in excellent condition get the highest rents. It's advisable to ignore these extremely high and low values unless your unit meets the requirements for an outlier. To find the average rental rate, only consider rents in the middle range. To get a reasonable monthly rent amount for your property, use this rental rate. Avoid the temptation to overvalue your rental.

Determine a Reasonable ROI

You must divide your projected annual return by your investment to determine the ROI. Estimating the investment amount is not advisable. This is the entire sum of money you will need to purchase the home. The anticipated profit from renting the property is known as the annual return. To increase your return on investment (ROI), it can be tempting to overestimate your desired returns. To obtain an exact return on investment, you must maintain realism. Depending on your specific goal, the market, and your location, the desired ROI can change significantly.

If you haven't already purchased an investment rental property, you can determine its value beforehand. Start by calculating the property's potential earnings. Next, determine the type of return on investment you desire. Calculate the optimal buying price for the property by dividing your profit by the ROI percentage. If you can't afford the property, it's not worth the investment. If you can buy the house for less, it could be the best investment for you.

Conducting Property Inspection

Property inspections are thorough examinations of a rental property to determine its general condition. They are often carried out by property managers, landlords, or professional inspectors. These inspections have several uses, including spotting maintenance problems, recording damages, and guaranteeing that lease terms are being followed. A property inspector closely inspects many areas of the property, such as the appliances, overall cleanliness, electrical and plumbing systems, and structural stability. This thorough inspection helps in locating any maintenance issues, lease violations, and safety risks.

Types of Rental Inspections

Different time periods and levels of thoroughness are essentially what we mean when we refer to different sorts of rental inspections. Below, we'll go over the five most typical types of inspections and what you should check for each time.

Move-In Inspections: These inspections are conducted when a new tenant comes into a rental property. They entail taking pictures of the property before the tenant moves in. Landlords can make sure the renter is aware of any pre-existing damages and provide a baseline for comparisons in the future by performing a move-in check. A move-in checklist of some kind should be with the inspector during this inspection. This checklist allows you to take notes on the features and maintains track of everything that has to be evaluated. The inspector then writes a report that reflects the property's condition.

The tenant signs the checklist and report, which then constitute part of the lease. These records are then compared with the move-out inspection when it comes time to move out. This comparison may aid in determining what damages are considered unusual and can be deducted from the security deposit.

Routine Inspections: Routine inspections are carried out at regular intervals during a tenant's residence. Landlords can evaluate the state of the property, determine what needs to be maintained, and handle lease violations or tenant problems by conducting these inspections. Regular inspections facilitate continued contact between renters and landlords. They can also be done more frequently if the landlord feels the renter is violating any of the provisions of the lease agreement. This could entail bringing in unapproved pets or roommates into the rented home.

It is especially vital to ensure that you do not violate the tenant's right to "quiet enjoyment" of the premises. In order to accomplish this, you must abide by all applicable local, state, and federal laws and ensure that the renter is informed prior to any inspections.

However, telling a renter of an inspection may make them feel as if they are being accused of something wrong. Then, you should reassure them that they are only standard inspections and that the objective is to evaluate the rental property's condition. This gives them enough time to repair any flaws or damages that would otherwise appear on the inspection report.

Drive-By Inspections: A drive-by inspection is one that is conducted without entering the property itself. Most of the time, especially on the weekends or in the evenings, rental property owners or property managers will merely do a visual check of the exterior of the building. The primary objective of these examinations is to identify any anomalies. For instance, there may be a pet on the property if you see a dog in the yard or perhaps hear barking as you're driving by. You can now arrange a regular check-up, but don't jump to the conclusion that the tenant is keeping pets against their will.

During these inspections, communicating with neighbors is another approach to acquiring information. Neighbors are usually a fantastic way to evaluate your tenant's behavior and discover if there is any misconduct.

Move-Out Property Inspection: Move-out inspections are to be carried out when the tenant is ready to vacate the premises. The day the tenant vacates the property should be the date of this kind of examination. It is crucial that the inspection be completed quickly following the tenant's departure. If not, the tenant may claim that the damage was not their fault. It's crucial to let the tenant know about anything that needs to be done before the inspection. It is important to inform them that the outcome of this inspection will dictate whether they receive their full security deposit returned or a portion of it.

The move-out inspection ought to adhere to a checklist, just like the move-in inspection. This checklist, which compares the property's condition, should be the same as the move-in checklist.

Change in Ownership: A change of ownership inspection is the final category of inspections for rental properties. When a property owner employs a new landlord, property manager, or property management company, this type of examination is conducted. When selecting a new property management company, it is best to allow them to do their own property inspection. This will spare them from having to rely on potentially inaccurate reports from the previous company.

Generally speaking, this inspection is far more extensive and includes far more than a standard inspection. It also lists any issues and things that need to be maintained on the property.

How Inspection is Conducted
Now that you've informed your renters and made arrange-ments for the inspection, it's time to dig in and get to work. Performing comprehensive inspections is a crucial component of efficient property management. In order to make sure that your property stays in excellent condition, you should inspect both the interior and exterior of the building to find any problems or places that require maintenance.

Exterior Inspection: When performing an outside inspection, pay close attention to the property's exterior features and surroundings. Start by carefully inspecting the building's facade, looking for any indications of damage or deterioration. If you see any peeling paint, loose siding, or cracks, they could need to be repaired. Additionally, look for any leaks or missing shingles on the roof. Keep in mind that a well-kept exterior guards against any structural damage in addition to improving the property's curb appeal.

Then turn your attention to the outdoor spaces and landscaping. Inspect the driveway, sidewalks, and lawn's state. Keep an eye out for any hazards to safety, such as overgrown plants, cracks in the pavement, or uneven surfaces. Inspect decks, patios, and fences, among other exterior structures, for indications of deterioration. Proper management of these locations guarantees that your residential tenants can safely enjoy the outdoor spaces.

Interior Inspection: Now let's move on to the interior inspection. Bring your checklist and any required tools and enter the property. Start by inspecting each room, beginning with the living area. Take note of the state of the ceiling, floors, and walls. Keep an eye out for any water damage, stains, or cracks that could need to be fixed. To make sure windows are working properly, open and close them and look for any leaks or drafts.

Make your way to the restrooms and kitchen. Examine the cabinets, plumbing fittings, and appliances. To make sure everything functions properly, check the water pressure, flush the toilets, and turn on the taps. Keep an eye out for any indications of leaks, mold, or broken fixtures that require replacement or repair. Remember to check the bedrooms as well. Look for any indications of pest infestations, including mouse droppings or bed bugs. Make sure all of the locks and doors are in good working order to provide your tenants with a sense of security.

Document Findings - It is essential that you carefully record your observations while you perform the property inspection. Make thorough notes of any problems or areas that need care. Take pictures or videos to show the state of the property with visual aids. This paperwork will serve as a guide when talking about repairs or resolving tenant issues.

It's time to take care of any problems or repairs that have been found during the property inspection. In the next part, we'll look at ways to handle these issues and maintain the best possible condition for your property.

Dealing with Repairs and Issues

Managing problems and repairs is crucial when owning rental property in order to guarantee the happiness and well-being of both landlords and tenants. This portion of the property inspection process is essential to keeping a safe and functional living environment since it helps discover issues and schedule repairs.

Identifying Problems: Inspections require a good eye for recognizing potential faults. Whether it's a cracked window, a leaky faucet, or a broken electrical outlet, recognizing these problems enables property owners to take preventative action and fix them before they worsen and require more expensive repairs.

Addressing Maintenance Issues: Once problems are detected, it is critical to fix maintenance issues as soon as possible to avoid further damage and tenant dissatisfaction. It is crucial to have a trustworthy network of qualified contractors and repair specialists. Property owners should have a list of reliable individuals and companies that can quickly handle a variety of maintenance needs, from electricians to plumbers. A network guarantees the best possible quality and expedites turnaround times for repairs. A property management services firm can be useful for maintenance and other repairs because they have a large network of professionals that can assist with these tasks.

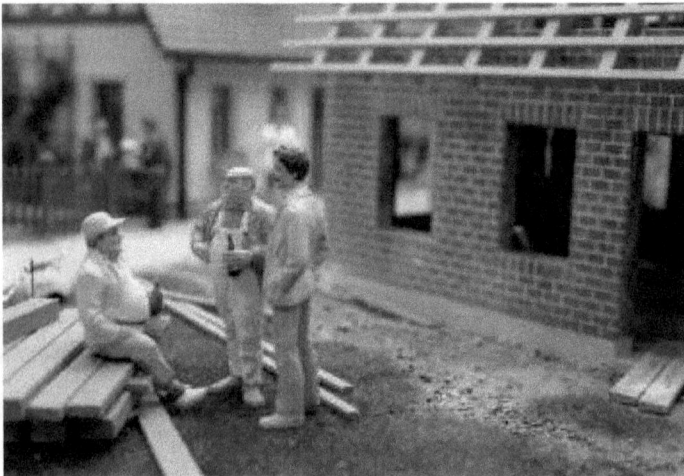

Schedule Repairs: The next stage is to schedule repairs after maintenance issues have been identified and addressed. Tenants and contractors should collaborate closely with property owners to choose the best time to do repairs. This guarantees that the tenants' daily lives are not unduly disturbed and makes it possible for repairs to be finished quickly. Clear and effective communication is essential when scheduling repairs. Tenants should be notified of the estimated time of completion and status of repairs, and landlords should provide them advance notice. Advance notification helps to establish trust and maintain a strong landlord-tenant relationship.

By swiftly resolving issues and scheduling repairs, property owners demonstrate their dedication to preserving the property's condition and assuring tenant contentment. This proactive strategy helps you manage your property more successfully overall and ultimately saves time and money.

CHAPTER FOUR
FINANCING YOUR RENTAL INVESTMENT

Real estate is undoubtedly the oldest type of investment, but it wasn't until the late twentieth century that financing a home became a must for the majority of Americans. This is particularly true for individuals wishing to participate in the real estate market in order to develop and diversify their portfolios, create passive income, or buy their first house. Knowing your financing options is crucial, whether you're an experienced investor or a novice, since you'll need to make sure your profits exceed the interest you'll have to pay.

Investment in property is a desirable endeavor for anyone seeking to increase their wealth and income due to its numerous benefits. The possibility of appreciation is one of the main justifications, since property values usually rise with time and offer substantial capital gains when sold.

Exploring Financial Options

Investment property finance is becoming increasingly sophisticated and diverse. While conventional mortgages are still popular for this purpose, you have access to a variety of alternative financing choices, including hard money loans, private money lenders, crowdfunding platforms, and syndicates.

Traditional Mortgages

Traditional mortgages are available to individuals and families looking to purchase a primary residence. Usually, these loans have set interest rates and are repaid over a period of 15 to 30 years. Conventional mortgages are secured by the asset being bought. If the borrower fails to make payments, the lender may foreclose on the property.

The term traditional mortgage refers to any mortgage that isn't funded or guaranteed by federal program. But it might not always be the best option for you, so make sure you talk to a mortgage lender or broker; they will run the numbers for you and make sure you find out exactly how much you can afford, what your down payment needs to be, and areas where you can improve to get the house of your dreams. Also, keep in mind that a larger down payment or a better credit score can help you get the home of your dreams. Remember, too, that different lenders offer different eligibility requirements, so do your homework and find one that connects with you.

Conventional Loans

If you own your primary residence, you are probably familiar with conventional financing. A typical mortgage follows rules established by Freddie Mac or Fannie Mae. Unlike loans from the Federal Home Administration, the Department of Veterans Affairs, or the Department of Agriculture, they are not backed by the federal government. Conventional financing typically requires a down payment of 20% of the purchase price of the home, though many lenders may accept less, based on your income and credit. With an investment property, however, lenders frequently demand a down payment of 30% of its purchase price.

A conventional loan's approval and interest rate are determined by your credit score and history. Lenders also look at your assets and income. You will have to show your ability to pay off any debt, including a mortgage on your house, as well as the monthly loan payments on an investment property. Debt-to-income ratios do not account for future rental income, and most lenders require you to have a minimum of six months' worth of cash on hand to pay off your loan in the event that you do not receive any income from the property. The following are the main categories of traditional bank loans:

- *Adjustable-rate mortgages*: These loans have variable monthly payments since their initial lower fixed rate of interest is followed by periodic adjustments dependent on market conditions.
- *Fixed-rate mortgages*: These feature a fixed interest rate and monthly payment for the duration of the loan, which provides stability and predictability for long-term financial planning.
- *Jumbo loans*: Usually used to purchase high-value houses, these loans surpass the Federal Housing Fina-

nce Agency's loan limitations. Their interest rates are higher, and their credit standards are more stringent.

Pros and Cons

One of the key benefits of conventional loans is that they have lower interest rates than other types of funding, such as hard money loans. In the long run, this makes them more economical. Furthermore, conventional loans have longer payback terms—typically between 15 and 30 years. Lower monthly payments and a more controllable cash flow could arise from this.

Stricter qualifying standards, such as lower debt-to-income ratios, higher credit scores, and a substantial amount of documentation, are frequently attached to these loans. Some may find it difficult to qualify as a result. The demand for bigger down payments—typically 30% or more—presents another difficulty and may act as a deterrent for investors lacking substantial financial reserves.

Private Financing

Private loans are those made from one person to another. A private money loan often comes from an investor's friends and relatives. If you don't have any friends or family who can lend you money for an investment property, consider attending local real estate investment networking events.

The actual loan terms and interest rates for private money loans might range from exceedingly beneficial to predatory, depending on your relationship with the lender. These loans are often secured by a formal agreement that allows the lender to seize the property if you fail to make payments. If you are new to real estate investment, think about how your relationship with the person who loaned you private money will suffer if you default before you get started.

Pros and Cons

Private money loan approval processes are frequently more expeditious and lenient, which facilitates the acquisition of financing—even for those with imperfect credit.

Due to the higher risk that private lenders incur, these loans frequently have higher interest rates and costs than conventional bank loans. This is a major disadvantage. In addition, there can be less supervision and protection for you because the loans are not governed by conventional financial institutions. Finally, even the finest financial prospects might not be worth the deal and its personal consequences if you're borrowing from friends or relatives.

Commercial Loans

Commercial loans are an important source of funding for those looking to purchase multi-unit residential homes, commercial properties, or mixed-use developments. These loans have unique guidelines, advantages, and difficulties that set them apart from residential mortgages.

Commercial loans are used to fund real estate holdings with a business focus, including apartment complexes, office buildings, retail stores, warehouses, and mixed-use sites. They are not meant for owner-occupied or single-family houses. In contrast to residential mortgages, terms for commercial loans are often shorter, ranging from five to twenty years, and they may include amortization periods that go beyond the original loan term. At the conclusion of the loan's term, a balloon payment—a big sum—may also be required.

Pros and Cons

Commercial loans are ideal for funding large-scale real estate projects such as multifamily apartment buildings and mixed-use developments. These loans frequently have greater borrowing restrictions, enabling investors to purchase more expensive properties. Furthermore, extended repayment terms offered by commercial loans may lead to reduced monthly payments and better cash flow. Commercial loan interest rates can be competitive as well, particularly if you have a strong company strategy and excellent credit.

One of the primary downsides of commercial loans is there more stringent requirements. Usually, you need a lot of paperwork to qualify, such as thorough financial records and company plans. Furthermore, greater down payments are frequently required for commercial loans, which can be a considerable financial commitment.

Additionally, the lengthy approval process may keep you out of some real estate transactions. Finally, due to the higher risk involved in investing in commercial real estate, commercial loans may have higher interest rates and costs than resid-ential ones.

Federal Housing Administration (FHA) Loan

The Federal Housing Administration, a division of the United States Department of Housing and Urban Development, insures mortgages, and an FHA loan is one such mortgage. FHA loans are frequently an excellent choice for first-time home purchasers, those with low savings, and those with credit difficulties because they require a minimum 3.5% down payment for borrowers with a credit score of 580 or above.

Even if you have filed for bankruptcy or don't satisfy the standards for a conventional mortgage, you can still be eligible for an FHA loan. The federal government does not provide FHA loans, but it does insure them. Because of the insurance, FHA lenders are ready to give borrowers who might not be eligible for traditional Private lenders who have received approval from the FHA to make FHA loans include numerous banks, credit unions, and nonbanks (a particular category of lender).

Several different kinds of residences can be purchased or refinanced with an FHA housing loan, including:

- Single-family homes.
- Multifamily residences with two to four units.
- Condominium units.
- Certain manufactured dwellings (fixed on a stable base).

Renovations to an existing house or new construction can also be financed with certain FHA loan programs. All properties, though, no matter how new or existing, have to go through an FHA appraisal. An FHA loan can be used to purchase (or refinance) a home if it satisfies government requirements. Home loan better terms in the event of a default.

Understanding Mortgage Rates and Terms

A mortgage's term refers to how long a lender will lend mortgage funds to a borrower for. This period is most commonly two to five years, but it can range from six months to ten years. In general, an interest rate will be lower and the cost of borrowing money will be lower depending on the mortgage period. You will either settle the outstanding sum at the conclusion of each term or renegotiate the mortgage for an extended period of time until the full amount is paid back.

Paying off your mortgage in full might take a long period, typically 15 to 25 years. Amortization is the process of paying back your debt in full over a predetermined length of time by making principal and interest payments in installments. Mortgage lenders have recently extended amortization durations to 30, 35, and 40 years.

Short Term
Short-term agreements, such as mortgage contracts, typically last two years or less. Compared to longer terms, short-term mortgages have lower borrowing costs (interest rates). A short-term mortgage is usually chosen by those who think

that interest rates are greater now than they will be later. When it comes time for renewal, they expect interest rates to drop.

Long Term

Typically, long-term contracts last three years or longer. Long-term mortgages are slightly more expensive than short-term mortgages, so the interest rate will be higher. A higher interest rate appeals to borrowers who appreciate the stability and predictability of fixed expenses over time. A consistent mortgage payment provides peace of mind and makes budgeting simpler.

There are numerous approaches to mortgage repayment. A predetermined fixed rate is comforting to some people since it makes budgeting and other life plans easier. Some people might prefer greater repayment flexibility; their situation may involve varying cash flow, and they may wish to make larger installments whenever it is feasible. Different mortgages appeal to various types of borrowers. Your mortgage profess-sional can assist you in determining what is best for your situation.

Rates

The interest rate on a loan is the total amount of interest charged, expressed as a percentage. It is determined by either the rate at which the Bank of the United States charges lenders to make loans, or by bond yields. Interest rates are typically higher for longer loan terms, and they decrease for shorter terms. The interest and principal payments are combined into one regular mortgage payment, which is known as a "blended principal and interest payment".

Fixed Rate Mortgage

Your interest rate won't fluctuate during the course of the mortgage if you accept a fixed rate mortgage. There are never any surprises because you will always be aware of the exact amount of your payments and the total amount of your mortgage that will be paid off by the end of the term. The lender will often offer a renewal at the end of the term, with a choice of a new term and the interest rate that is in effect at that time, provided there is still a balance and time left on your amortization period.

Variable/Adjustable Rate Mortgage

A variable rate mortgage is one in which you consent to a varying interest rate for the term of the loan. Interest rates can change from month to month and are based on the prime lending rate set by the bank. Your payment amount stays the same, but the amount applied to the principal changes when interest rates fluctuate. For instance, as interest rates fall, a larger portion of your mortgage payment gets applied towards the total amount owed. Certain lenders have auto-mated adjustments to the payment amount to reflect changes in the interest component of the payment in the event that the interest rate fluctuates.

When the prime interest rate fluctuates, the payment on an adjustable rate mortgage will also automatically alter. By doing this, it will be guaranteed that each payment will contri-bute enough to the main balance to pay off the mortgage at the conclusion of the amortization period. It's crucial for the borrower to know if the payment will alter automatically or if it will stay the same when the interest rate fluctuates, regardless of whether your lender calls it an adjustable rate mortgage or a variable rate mortgage. Homeowners who think interest rates will eventually decline from their present high level should consider an adjustable rate mortgage, often known as a variable rate mortgage.

Budgeting for Property Expenses

While owning and maintaining a rental property has its advantages, there are significant financial obligations involved. Maintaining the profitability of your property depends on your ability to comprehend and efficiently manage a variety of charges, including mortgage payments and maintenance. Landlords work hard to keep their homes in good condition and run their rental businesses effectively. However, the profitability of a landlord is limited by rising taxes, mortgage payments, and maintenance expenses. Here are seven typical costs associated with rental properties and how landlords should plan for them:

Mortgage Payments
Since buying rental properties usually involves a large cash outlay, most investors take out loans and mortgages. Even though your mortgage will probably be your biggest ongoing expense as a landlord, it's crucial to realize that, particularly

in regions with lower rental rates or during recessionary times, it's not always feasible to set rent high enough to cover these payments. You must therefore make sure you can afford the mortgage payments without depending entirely on rental revenue before selecting an investment property. This strategy aids in protecting against problems with cash flow. Properties with positive cash flow, where net rental revenue surpasses all costs, including mortgage payments, are what investors should strive for.

This approach pays for itself and increases the return on your investment. Investors may also look into refinancing options to achieve cheaper rates and safeguard their investments during periods of rising interest rates. This, though, needs to be a component of a more comprehensive financial plan that prioritizes affordability and steady cash flow.

Maintenance and Repairs

Maintenance and repairs are an important component of property management that landlords frequently perceive as a major source of stress. According to 50% of respondents in our most recent LinkedIn community study, it's the most difficult aspect of property management.

Budgeting tips

Owners of rental properties should set aside enough money for maintenance in order to guarantee efficient operations. There are a few general guidelines that can help in cost estimation:

- The 50% rule states that you should set aside half of your monthly rental income for upkeep, repairs, and other costs associated with your property.
- The "1% rule" suggests that yearly upkeep expenses could represent 1% of the property's overall worth.
- *Square footage rule*: The size of the property can also be used to estimate maintenance expenditures.
- *General budgeting recommendations*: One to four percent of the property's annual value should be set aside for upkeep. This assists in paying for a range of charges, such as regular upkeep, unforeseen repairs, and one-time expenses for things like waste disposal, pest treatment, and HVAC filter replacements.

Types of Maintenance

Furthermore, there are various maintenance concerns that landlords should plan for and be ready for at all times:

- When something urgently has to be replaced or repaired, emergency maintenance is necessary. This can include fixing any plumbing or electrical problems in order to maintain the property secure and livable.
- Preventive maintenance, such as arranging routine air conditioner cleaning to remove debris and lubricate moving parts, aims to minimize unforeseen problems and keep a property in good operating order at all times.
- Seasonal maintenance is carried out at predetermined times that should ideally correspond with the varying

seasons. This covers tasks like clearing snow and cleaning gutters.

Before renting out the apartment to a new tenant, landlords should take care of small maintenance tasks like painting and carpet cleaning after tenants vacate.

Utilities

Utility costs are a crucial factor in property management. These costs include garbage collection, gas, electricity, water, and sewage. These are usually monthly deductible costs. The approach to dealing with these fees varies depending on the landlord's preferences and the circumstances of the rental agreement.

Landlords may choose to include utility bills in the rental price in certain situations. As property owners, they are responsible for paying their utility bills directly. This type of arrangement can be especially desirable in rental markets where all-inclusive leases are more tempting to tenants, or in multi-unit buildings where individual utility metering would not be feasible. In order to offset these expenditures, landlords that select this option usually include the utilities bills in the rental prices.

Alternatively, landlords may choose to charge their renters for the utilities costs. Tenants bear the responsibility of establishing utility company accounts and making payments for the services rendered. This method is frequently used in single-family rental properties or other settings where it is simple to measure and assign specific tenant usage to individual utilities.

Property Management
Investors who are unable or would prefer not to handle their rental properties themselves may find it advantageous to hire a property manager. Daily responsibilities for property managers include coordinating maintenance, communicating with tenants, collecting rent, and responding to any emergencies or issues from tenants. They can also help with leasing and tenant screening, making sure the property attracts and keeps trustworthy occupants.

Usually, property management services cost between 7 and 10% of the monthly rent. Even though this expense is considerable, the landlord's considerable time and effort savings frequently outweigh it. For landlords who have numerous properties or who live far from their rental homes, property managers can be very helpful as they provide the knowledge and tools needed to handle various elements of property management effectively.

Expert property managers may offer helpful market insights and guidance on legal compliance, assisting in navigating the complexities of local rental rules and regulations, in addition to the practical aspects of property maintenance and tenant management.

Hiring a property manager ultimately comes down to personal circumstances, such as the landlord's availability, level of experience, and size of rental business. Many landlords find that the convenience, know-how, and assurance provided by reputable property management firms make their investment worthwhile since it frees them up to concentrate on other personal and professional obligations or more ambitious investment plans.

Insurance

Get the right landlord insurance to safeguard your investment, whether you're a seasoned real estate investor or a first-time landlord. Specifically tailored for hazards associated with rental properties, landlord insurance is distinct from traditional homeowner's insurance in a number of ways.

The greater coverage provided by landlord insurance frequently justifies the 20% premium increase over homeowner's insurance. This kind of insurance protects landlords against monetary losses brought on by damage to their property, legal obligations, and other hazards specific to renting out a space.

The following categories of coverage are typically included in typical landlord insurance policies:

- o *Property protection*: This includes harm to the actual property brought on by a variety of events, such as storms, fires, vandalism, or damage from occupants. It may also cover other structures on the land, like sheds or garages, in addition to the building itself.
- o *Liability protection*: Liability insurance is essential for shielding the landlord from court cases or lawsuits

resulting from accidents or property damage. In the event that a tenant or guest is hurt as a result of poor property upkeep, this may include hospital expenses or legal fees.

o *Revenue loss coverage*: Some plans protect against the loss of rental revenue. For example, this coverage can reimburse the landlord for lost rent while repairing or reconstructing a property after an insured loss renders it uninhabitable.

Landlord plans can also be tailored with extra coverages to meet certain requirements or dangers. For instance, since ordinary plans frequently do not cover natural disasters like wildfires, floods, or earthquakes, landlords may choose to obtain specific coverage in such areas.

Landlords should carefully evaluate their insurance needs, taking into account several aspects such as the location of the property, the kind of rental, and their own level of risk tolerance. Speaking with an insurance expert can help you choose which coverage alternatives are best for you.

Comprehensive landlord insurance is more than simply a safety precaution; it's an investment in peace of mind. It guarantees that in the event of unforeseen circumstances, such as property damage or legal problems, landlords won't be left to shoulder the entire financial burden.

Property Taxes
The local government sets the property taxes that are assessed on the owner of the leased property. The sum varies

greatly depending on the locality and is usually determined by the assessed value of the property. In addition to making sure that the assessment of their property is correct and equitable, landlords must be aware of the local property tax rate. Regularly examining and, if required, challenging tax assessments can help prevent overpayments. Since property taxes are a constant item that is unaffected by rental income, they should be taken into account when creating the overall budget.

Rental Income Taxes

However, the amount of tax on rental income is determined by how much is made by renting out the property. This is taxable income, according to the IRS, and needs to be reported every year. By using numerous deductions for the costs of upkeep and operation of the rental property, landlords can lower their taxable income. Included in them are depreciation, property management fees, repair and maintenance costs, mortgage interest, and insurance payments.

To properly report rental revenue and maximize subsequent permissible tax deductions, accurate and comprehensive documentation of all expenses and income must be kept throughout the year. Speaking with a tax expert can help you manage rental income taxes efficiently, make sure you're following the law, and maximize your tax savings.

CHAPTER FIVE
LEGAL CONSIDERATION AND DOCUMENTATION

Understanding Landlord-Tenant Laws

Tenant-landlord relationships are a fundamental feature of the real estate market, and they are regulated by a body of laws intended to safeguard each party's obligations and rights. Understanding the fundamentals of landlord-tenant legislation is essential, whether you are a landlord trying to lease property or a renter searching for a place to live.

Lease Agreements

The lease agreement provides the foundation for the landlord-tenant relationship. This legally binding agreement specifies the tenancy's terms and conditions, such as the rent amount, payment schedule, lease period, and any other rules or restrictions. Before signing, it is crucial that both parties carefully go over and comprehend the terms to make sure they are aware of their respective responsibilities.

The terms and conditions of the tenancy should be expressly stated in a well-drafted lease agreement, and these include:

- Property Description
- Security Deposit Detail
- Rules and Regulations
- Renewal/Termination Clauses
- Maintenance and Repairs
- Signature of Both Parties

Tenant Rights and Responsibilities

Tenants have a set of rights that protect their well-being and assure fair treatment. Here are some fundamental rights:

- o Tenants are entitled to a livable environment that satisfies fundamental health and safety requirements. Landlords bear the responsibility of resolving any concerns that impact habitability.

o Within their rented space, tenants are entitled to privacy, and landlords are required to give notice before accessing the property—with the exception of emergencies.

o Fair housing rules ban discriminatory behaviors; thus, tenants are protected from discrimination based on variables including race, gender, religion, or disability.

o Renters are entitled to the quiet enjoyment of their rental space, which means they can do so free from needless landlord interference.

The general tenants' responsibilities are intended to protect the property and the landlord's investment. Tenants not only help to maintain the property's condition and worth, but they also create an ideal living environment that benefits all parties involved. These obligations, which specify what tenants may and may not do while using the rental property, will be made explicit in the terms of the lease agreement.

Additional general responsibilities expected include:

o *Meeting payment responsibilities*: Tenants are accountable for paying utilities and rent on time when they sign a rental agreement.

o *Repairing damages*: Tenants should be responsible for fixing or covering the cost of any damage to the property that results from events other than standard wear and tear.

o *Disturbances*: Tenants are urged to refrain from disturbing their neighbors with excessive noise so that everyone can enjoy the premises.

- o *Permitting landlord access*: Landlords are entitled to access their properties in order to conduct inspections. Tenants have to let them in, but you have to tell them when and where you are coming.
- o *Vacating property at the conclusion of the lease term*: When the lease expires, tenants must depart the premises on that day. Additionally, tenants have to vacate the property in good shape.

Steps to take when Tenants Violates

Landlords are required by law to follow certain procedures in handling situations where a tenant violates the terms of their lease or the law. The most important thing is to communicate. Landlords should engage in open and productive communication with tenants to address the issue and find a solution. In numerous cases, effective communication can help overcome misunderstandings or problems.

If communication fails, landlords should study their lease agreement to understand its rights and remedies. Landlords may be required to provide written warnings or notices to tenants, precisely describing the issue and the required corrective activities, based on the type and seriousness of the violation. These notices should adhere to state and local legislation and include appropriate compliance deadlines.

Landlords may be required to launch legal actions in more serious situations, such as nonpayment of rent or major lease violations. This usually entails following state-specific eviction regulations and deadlines and filing for eviction through the proper legal channels. Landlords should consult with legal practitioners that specialize in landlord-tenant law to make sure that all legal requirements are met during the process of eviction.

Security Deposits

Security deposits play an important part in landlord-tenant relationships. States have their own regulations for collecting, using, and returning security deposits. To prevent disagreements at the end of the lease period, both parties should be informed of these state rules.

- Tenants may be required to provide a security deposit to landlords in order to cover any damages or unpaid rent.
- Security deposits are used to cover delinquent rent and damages over and above normal wear and tear.
- The security deposit should be held in a different account, and at the conclusion of the tenancy, the landlord shall give an itemized summary of all deductions.
- Landlords may withhold payments for delinquent rent, repairs that exceed normal wear and tear, and other permitted causes.
- Landlords are required to give written notice to tenants outlining any deductions they want to make from the security deposit, including any amounts they plan to withhold.

Requirement for Security Deposit

A security deposit can be more than the usual amount, which is one month's rent. The amount of the security deposit placed in escrow may not be enough if the rental rate on the property goes up. While security deposits are held, they may earn interest, but the rate of rent rises may outpace the interest. The tenant would then have to increase the amount stored in the security deposit.

Due to local legal requirements, security deposits are frequently treated as trust money and are not taxable income. However, security deposits used as final rent payments must be reported as advance rent and should be taxed when paid.

Special considerations

Certain states allow landlords to use security deposits as rent from non-paying tenants, or they can be used to cover damages committed by former tenants. When a tenant vacates a property, each state has laws governing the use of security deposits to cover the last month's rent. The last month's rent and a security deposit may not be the same and need to be paid separately, depending on local laws. If a security deposit is to be used as final rent, the landlord may even require the renter's written consent.

There may be issues with the amount necessary for security deposits in some cities or communities. There may be landlords in some districts who want larger security deposit amounts than in the neighborhood. This may have the unintended consequence of discouraging lower-class people and families from relocating to certain locations. Local legislation may be adopted to limit the size of a security deposit in relation to the rental price of a property.

Create Lease Agreements

A legally binding contract that specifies the terms and conditions for renting property is called a lease agreement, sometimes known as a rental agreement. It is signed by two parties. This agreement, which is usually utilized when renting out residential or commercial properties—like homes, offices, or apartments—ensures that the tenant and landlord are aware of their respective rights and obligations.

A lease agreement primarily involves the landlord, also known as the lessor, who is the owner of the property, and the tenant, also known as the lessee, who wants to rent it for a predetermined amount of time. To safeguard both parties'

interests and avert potential conflicts, a thorough leasing agreement must be drafted.

Content of Lease Agreement

- Names of lessors and lessees, or their agents.
- An explanation of the attribute.
- Rent amount, due dates, grace period, and late fees.
- Method of payment for rent.
- How to end the contract before its expiration date and any associated fees.
- The quantity of the security deposit and the account number that holds it.
- Utilities provided by the lessor and the method used to calculate the charge determine if there are lower fees for such utilities.
- The tenant is allowed to access all on-site amenities and facilities, including the laundry room, security systems, and swimming pool.
- Rules and restrictions include pet rules, noise rules, and penalties for violations.
- Indicate the availability of parking lots, including any designated spots, if any.
- The process for handling emergency requests and tenant repair requests.

Eviction Procedures

In some cases, landlords may need to commence eviction proceedings owing to nonpayment of rent, lease violations, or other justifiable causes.

Legal Grounds for Eviction: Generally speaking, landlords are only able to remove tenants for certain specific offenses, like failing to pay rent, breaking the conditions of the lease, or other legal grounds. It's crucial to provide good cause for the eviction.

Notice to Quit or Cure: Landlords must typically give the tenant a written notice outlining the grounds for eviction and, in certain situations, providing a chance to resolve the situation (make good on past-due rent payments, fix a lease violation, etc.). The length of notice varies depending on the eviction's cause and jurisdiction.

Filing an Eviction Case: If the tenant fails to comply with the notice to depart or cure, the landlord may file an eviction case in the relevant court, also known as an unlawful detainer action. The landlord must pay the filing fees and provide the appropriate documentation, including the notice given to the tenant.

Lease Terms and Conditions
A property needs to have a number of terms incorporated when leasing or renting it out. For example, if you agree to a tenancy for eleven months, one issue is how the notice of termination will be sent and when the tenancy will end. If the renter wishes to stay at the property longer, how and when should they notify you of this? What are the terms of the agreement? Will there be an increase in rent, and if so, by how much?

Will there be a one-time rent or lease increase if the lessee has signed a five-year contract? What kind of payment will be used, as well as how and when the rent is due each month? What is the set rent amount for the duration of the lease? If the property is rented out or leased. (Rental agreements are made differently than leases; there is a noticeable difference between the two).

Occupancy limit

How many people will be staying at the property should be specified in the leasing agreement. For instance, in India, visitors possess higher powers and can stay for as long as they like. This could lead to a group of people who were not included in the lease agreement occupying the property; yet, as they are visitors, they are not considered long-term members. But what happens if they plan to use the rental home for months at a time?

While it may not affect you as a lessor, society may object to it, and the use of your rental property may rise, increasing its wear and tear. Therefore, a full summary of the occupancy limits should be included in the lease agreements. By providing these details, you will be able to legally evict a renter who has subleased a portion of your unit to a friend or relative.

Movable assets

It is hard to handle every little detail when a property is rented out year-round in large cities due to the abundance of inhabitants that move about. But, if you wish to protect the movable assets within the property—furniture, wardrobes, ceiling fans, and so forth—make a list of everything and include it in the lease agreement along with a note about its terms and the amount of damage that will result in a fine. In this manner, any significant damage will be legally covered in the agreement, and you can recover their loss or damage from the last rent payment—even though you can allow for some wear and tear from usage.

Maintenance and repair

The upkeep and repairs of the property are a major source of disagreement for both the lessor and the lessee. After a year of tenancy, a tenant may need general maintenance before renewal or in-between tenancies, or they may want to paint the property, fix wardrobes or movable items, or both.

As a lessee, you may want to ensure that the provisions surrounding maintenance issues are clarified and that the lessor will handle them. In response, the lessor may offer similar ideas and work with others to find a compromise to address any such problems. Including these in the leasing agreement could facilitate greater communication and understanding between the parties.

CHAPTER SIX

PREPARING YOUR RENTAL PROPERTY

Renting your property is like allowing your adolescent to drive your car; you never know if it will return intact or with a missing wheel, fries between the seats, and a suspiciously broken side view mirror. Just like you can prepare your car for a potentially dangerous driver, you can also prepare your home for a strange new tenant. Whether you're thinking of renting out your house to make some extra cash or if you want to sell but the market is taking longer than you would like, don't go into it blindly.

Here are three things to think about before placing your house on the rental market:

- *It must be a current mortgage*: Examine your loan; there might be requirements for renting. For instance, you have to live in your house for a full year before renting if you have an FHA loan. If you are buying a home solely for rental purposes, you must notify your mortgage lender.
- *You must have saved up three months' worth of household expenses*: In the event that unexpected costs arise or the house doesn't rent as soon as you had

planned, this should cover everything (mortgage, bills, upkeep, etc.).

- *Consider hiring a property management company*: This is one chore that you may want to delegate to specialists. Property management firms handle the difficult aspects of renting a house on your behalf.

Making a good first impression is essential to drawing tenants to a rental property. Preparation is essential for guaranteeing that your rental property continually draws quality candidates whose profiles you are willing to accept as tenants into your property. Tenants desire to move into a place that seems tidy, secure, welcoming, and ready for use; frequently, their initial impression during a visit will determine whether or not they make this choice. Give your house the attention it deserves by staging it to look its best. Recall that you cannot change the initial impression a tenant has of your property when they see it for the first time.

Making Property Improvement

Although repairs and upgrades may appear to be interchangeable at first, there is an important distinction to be made for taxation purposes. While improvements enhance the property's worth or lengthen its useful life, repairs are required to keep it in good condition. For rental property owners to take advantage of tax discounts, deductions, credits, and other cost-saving measures, they must understand the distinction between the two.

The general goal of repairs for rental properties is to maintain the property habitable and compliant with all regulations, making sure that all major or structural components are in excellent functioning order. Any effort done to accomplish this is what the IRS defines as a repair.

Fixing a leaky roof is considered a repair based on the previously listed criteria, whereas replacing the entire roof is considered an improvement. Other instances include the following.

- Fixing a tap
- Repainting surfaces
- Fixing an air conditioner
- Maintaining the appliances

When comparing routine maintenance to capital renovations, the latter improves the property beyond its initial state. Among them are:

- Adding a new room
- Modernizing Appliances
- Changing the roof
- Installing a fresh HVAC system
- Renovating a restroom or kitchen
- Putting in new doors or windows
- Large maintenance projects that result in improvements (such as repairing a large pipe piece that takes up the entire kitchen floor)

Under the heading of capital expenditures, the cost in this instance would be categorized as a capital improvement.

An investment property can gain value through capital impro-vements, increasing its appeal to potential purchasers.

Furnishing and Staging Rentals

Make the most of the curb appeal of your rental property since first impressions count. Make sure the walks are clear, the outside lighting is functional, the lawn is kept up, and the landscaping is neat. Consider repainting the front door or having the entire exterior thoroughly cleaned. These tiny investments make a significant difference.

Decluttering and Depersonalization

Decluttering and depersonalizing the residence is one of the most crucial stages. Remove all debris to make rooms appear cleaner and more spacious. Remove souvenirs, artwork, and private images. Put away trinkets and specialized décor. This is supposed to be a place where potential tenants see themselves living, not where you live.

Clean and Repair

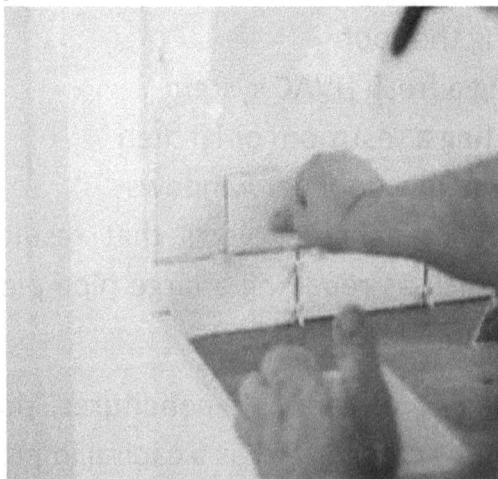

A bright, spotless home makes a lasting impression. Take care of any maintenance issues to keep your home in excellent shape. Resolve noisy doors, cracked tiles, and leaking faucets.

A property's overall quality is positively impacted by its level of maintenance. If you need assistance getting your house ready for a showing, your local real estate agent should be able to provide you with a list of reliable contractors to work with.

Highlight key Features and Selling points

When decluttering, make sure that desired features remain visible. For instance, place furniture to complement an open floor plan or draw attention to a beautiful fireplace. Draw attention to features such as huge closets, plenty of storage, laundry machines, and modern fixtures. Emphasize selling features like a big yard, a recently installed roof, or being close to parks.

Incorporate Neutral and Inviting Décor

To give the house a clean, modern appeal, use towels, accent cushions, drapes, and linens in neutral colors. Add useful furniture so that tenants can picture themselves using the room. For warmth, add a few green plants. For pleasant scents, try scented candles or a mild air refresher. The idea is to create a warm, inviting atmosphere.

Watch where the eye goes

There are quick and low-cost remedies to many of the minor issues that make a home appear shabbier than it should. As you move through each hallway and into each room, notice where your gaze is pulled. Even better, get an evaluative friend or relative to help. Take some "white out" and fill in any areas where the chipped white paint on the door frame draws your attention. Try hanging a picture to conceal the old nail holes in the wall if that's the problem.

Arrange Furniture Thoughtfully

Arrange furniture to showcase the flow and functionality of each room. Rooms can appear larger by clearing out excess furniture. Aim for a well-proportioned, aesthetically pleasing arrangement that compels potential buyers to explore the room.

Professional Photography

High-quality photographs are required for online listings. In order to present your house in the best possible light, try working with a professional photographer. First impressions count for a thousand words, and customers frequently see pictures first.

Setting Rental Prices

Making decisions and balancing multiple tasks are crucial aspects of real estate investing. While you may need to make judgments on the go and move from one duty to the next rapidly, there is one thing you should never rush: pricing your rental.

One of those factors that can significantly affect your profits is the cost of your renting. While an excessively high price may turn away potential tenants, the correct price might assist bring them in and, in some situations, help keep them renting for longer. Naturally, if it's too low, you run the danger of leaving money on the table.

In an attempt to rent out their properties as soon as possible, some landlords may set their rental prices unreasonably low. In an effort to swiftly recoup their investment, some can take the reverse approach and overcharge for their rents. Finding the sweet spot, however, or the price that is ideal for the market, the area, and your house itself—that is, not too high or too low—is crucial.

Pricing Strategy

Understand local rental trends: Setting prices starts with conducting a thorough market analysis. Start by examining local rental trends. Examine comparable homes on websites like Trulia and Zillow, then contrast the rental prices. By doing this, you can assess the state of the market and make sure your price is reasonable. Remember that the neighborhood can also have a big influence on the cost, with certain areas having higher rental prices than others. The cost may also be impacted by the availability of good schools, nearby facilities, and public transit. It can also be beneficial to find out what the average salary in the area is. Make sure your tenants can afford the rent, as you should usually make sure they are earning three times the amount you are asking.

Assessing property value: To build a firm foundation for deter-mining rental costs, accurately assess the value of your property. A property's value is mostly determined by its location, size, age, condition, and facilities. Thankfully, you can seek an expert for help with this. Consider contacting a professional appraiser to get an unbiased estimate of your property's value. Recall that while underpricing a rental property could result in lost income opportunities, over-pricing it might turn away prospective tenants. Aim for a fair rental price that corresponds to the current market value of your home.

Calculating operating expenses: Next, your rental should be treated like a commercial enterprise. Real estate investing entails monthly running fees for landlords. These should be covered by your rental income, which should also be sufficient for profit. Operating costs for rental properties could include:

- o Mortgage
- o Insurance
- o Property tax
- o Property management fees
- o Maintenance and repairs

While the market determines the rent, not your spending, running the figures might help you evaluate the profitability of your investment. For this reason, it's critical to precisely estimate your monthly expenses and set aside a percentage of your rental revenue to pay for them. It's also a good idea to set aside some cash for unforeseen emergencies or repairs. You may calculate the minimal rental price required to sustain positive cash flow by factoring in your expenses.

Rental market dynamics: It is essential to understand supply and demand dynamics in order to determine reasonable rental rates. Landlords may charge higher rents in a market with high demand and limited housing supply. On the other hand, you might need to lower your rental prices in order to draw in renters if the market is oversaturated with housing options.

Stay up to date on the state of the local market and be aware of any impending developments that might affect the demand for rentals. For instance, an employer moving to the region or the opening of new businesses nearby may enhance demand for housing, allowing you to raise your rental rates appropriately.

Adjusting to market fluctuation: Setting rent costs is not a one-time decision. Periodic modifications may be required to enhance returns and stay competitive as market conditions change. Keep an eye on changes in the rental market, assess how well your property is performing, and, when necessary, gradually raise your rental prices.

When considering a rent increase, keep your current tenants in mind. Frequent or excessive increases may result in tenant turnover, which can be costly and impede cash flow. Strike a balance that reflects shifts in the market and benefits long-term tenants. The best rent increases are usually those that are gradual but steady. Just make sure you are aware of any applicable local rent control legislation.

Rent Adjustment Consideration
When making rent adjustment decisions, many situations will be considered, depending on where you are in the develop-

ment of your portfolio. Let's say, for instance, that this is your first year renting an apartment. If so, your circumstances will have changed from years two, three, five, or ten since your portfolio might have expanded and your clientele might have been more diverse. When this occurs, it's critical to comprehend market economics in addition to the trends and desires specific to any property.

Rental market analysis: It is essential for landlords and property managers to be up to date on local and regional rental trends. Conducting routine rental market research will assist you in determining whether your current rental rates are competitive and what comparable properties in the area are asking for rent.

Demand and supply dynamics: Understanding demand and supply for rental properties in a target market is also a smart idea, and to properly get a hold on your data, you should evaluate aspects like population growth, employment patterns, and new development projects. Understanding the current and future situation of these variables will help you decide which approach is best for your rental property. It can also assist in identifying opportunities to suit the needs of prospective tenants and property investments.

Occupancy rates: Another great practice is to monitor the market as a whole and the occupancy rates of your properties specifically. You can then modify rents in accordance with the demand and any possible effects on vacancy rates. With this information, you can make sure that your properties are in great demand at all times and maintain your competitive edge.

Tenant retention: Consider the expense of turnover and balance it against prospective rental increases. Keeping current tenants and avoiding hefty rent increases may be more cost-effective than finding new ones.

Rental property amenities and conditions: Examine the state of your property and the amenities or services provided to tenants before opting to raise the rent. Assess whether any recent upgrades call for a raise or whether properties need to be modernized to meet the demands of the rental market. Through a thorough analysis of these variables, you can make sure your rental rates are reasonable.

Comparable property analysis: Comparing your homes' features and facilities to those of similar providers is crucial to keeping them competitive. You may maximize occupancy rates and rental income by adjusting your rent based on this analysis to reflect the relative appeal of your properties.

Inflation and economic indicators: It's always a good idea for business managers to monitor economic indicators and inflation because they have a big impact on operating costs. This will help ensure that your company remains lucrative and sustainable in the long run by increasing rental rates as needed.

Lease expiration timing: Understanding when your leases expire allows you to make strategic rental adjustments since it opens up discussion with tenants at a time when they expect change. It fosters fairness. In the event that a tenant switches, it also gives you more time to advertise new unit availability and fill your pipeline efficiently at a higher rate.

Tenant income levels: As a landlord, you must assess your tenants' income levels. If you must raise rents, try making gradual modifications to avoid putting tenants financially at risk. Taking these things into consideration makes things advantageous for both you and your tenants.

Tenant attitude and lifestyle: Non-monetary value can be defined as value received by the landlord from renters in a form other than rental income. Perhaps you have a calm, mature couple living on the property. They take good care of the outside and inside of the house, get along with the neighbors, and cause very little wear and tear on the property. They might pay $2,500 a month, and the property could be worth $3,000; however, in order to get that $3,000, you might have to rent to less responsible renters. There is value in having a tenant who is peaceful, dependable, and low maintenance.

Variety in rent increase: Each tenancy is distinct, and each tenant's relationship with you, the landlord, is also unique. It's not necessary to make a general announcement regarding all of your tenancies when you decide to raise your rents. Maybe the multi-resident renter who brings the trash cans to the curb every week can avoid getting a raise while the other tenants in the building get a notice. You can decide which tenants will receive the rent increase and which won't.

Competitor analysis: Keeping up with the rental tactics and pricing schemes of your rivals is essential if you're a property owner. By analyzing the market, you may position your properties to be competitive while remaining profitable. You may stay ahead of the competition in the market by keeping a watch on their actions and using that information to inform your own judgments about prices and marketing tactics.

Regulatory environment: Understanding regional compliance is essential when renting or leasing properties. By doing this, one can stay out of legal trouble and keep up good relations with both the real estate community and prospective tenants.

Renovation and upgrades: Highlighting the new features of a property you've just updated or remodeled is a wonderful strategy for justifying a higher rental price. The focus is on increased value. This is advantageous to you as the landlord as well as improving your tenants' quality of life in general. Thus, don't be afraid to make improvements to your property; think about the possibility of higher rent.

Financial modeling: Use financial models to forecast the effect of rent increases on your property's overall performance. This information can be used to assess the trade-offs between rising rents and the possible danger of increased vacancies.

Communication strategy: Responding quickly and honestly to tenant issues and inquiries will help you create trust and guarantee a seamless transition to new rent rates. When and how you begin your communication is equally critical, so prepare to design a marketing communications timeline alongside rent increase implementation.

Long-term strategy: Always think about how anything will affect the value of your properties and the portfolio's overall financial situation. This strategy makes sure that rent modifications are made with the portfolio's long-term interests in mind, rather than merely the short term.

Intended property goals: Lastly, and maybe most importantly, think about how long you want to invest. What are your objectives for the property, and how will increasing the rent impact them? Your approach and whether or not you decide to increase rent may vary depending on when you plan to sell the property or move back in. Fitting your plan to your objectives is essential.

CHAPTER SEVEN

ADVERTISING AND MARKETING YOUR RENTALS

Trying to find a new tenant might be difficult. It takes time, and the possibility of a costly vacant period always exists. However, you can simply, inexpensively, and most importantly, rapidly get your listing in front of thousands of potential tenants by utilizing a combination of traditional rental property promotion strategies and contemporary online marketing.

Crafting Effective Market Listing

A vacant rental property is an expensive problem until you locate a new tenant to pay the rent. However, informing people that your property is available is more complicated than simply scribbling down some statistics and publishing them on a couple of websites.

To make your investment property stand out from the competition, an efficient rental property listing needs a few essential components. Potential tenants will scroll past your listing until they locate their new rental property owned by another investor if it does not draw in the interest of your target rental market.

Draft an Attention-grabbing Headline

An attention-grabbing headline is the first step towards creating a superb rental listing for those pursuing other listings on their phones. Your headline serves as the hook, so make it count. Consider what makes your property special or appealing, then incorporate that information into your headline. Is there a well-known landmark in the area close to your rental? Does it have an amazing view of the water? Whatever it is, be sure to have a clear, descriptive headline.

Tenants will be drawn in by an attention-grabbing headline and be encouraged to click through to your entire listing. Here are a few instances:

- "Newly Renovated 3-Bedroom Townhome Close to Downtown"
- "Pet-Friendly Home for Rent with Fenced Backyard"

Once you've decided on a headline, you may go into greater detail in your description and use images to highlight what you have to offer. Don't forget your contact information. Tenants will require information on how to contact you in order to make an appointment for a showing or ask questions. One may also include a quick summary of the rental requirements, and it is important to consistently observe fair housing laws and regulations.

Be Descriptive

Without being unduly wordy, your rental listing should include a detailed description of the property. A few phrases that provide the essential "411" are unlikely to grab the interest of your potential tenant. The rental market for homes can frequently be fiercely competitive. What distinguishes your property from others? The listing should highlight the special features of your property in a way that draws interest and motivates a prospective tenant to submit an application.

When describing your property, don't forget to include:

- o The specifics (such as location, square footage, and the number of bedrooms and bathrooms)
- o Qualities and facilities
- o Details on the neighborhood, including its parks, restaurants, schools, and highway accessibility
- o The amount of rent due each month and any necessary fees

Focus on your Photos

Pictures are vital because if your title or pricing point catches tenants' interest, they will click through your photos before reading your description. Make sure you have a ton of pictures and that they are as professional as possible.

Tenants should be able to see what life might be like by looking at the photos that go with your listing. You want them to picture themselves moving in immediately. Showcase your kitchen by taking close-up photographs of the appliances, floors, and countertops. Add pictures of dens, living rooms, and any other areas your tenants plan to host guests. The bedroom photos are also crucial. Take pictures of the closet and any additional available storage. Remember to highlight your bathrooms as well as any outside areas, garages, and other unique features.

Use a nice camera, even if it's on your phone. Concentrate on the lighting and employ the perfect angles to make your property appear larger, cleaner, and more modern. Make sure to tidy up before the photoshoot. Nobody likes to see trash or mess. Nothing goes better with pictures than video. Adding a video to your ad allows you to provide potential renters with an up-to-date tour of your rental property. Create a video tour that takes potential buyers around the entire house starting at the front door.

Be a Storyteller
Not that you should publish a book about your rental house, per se. But a comprehensive, enjoyable to read listing will increase the appeal of your property significantly. Explain what a typical day looks like on your property. Prospective tenants are more interested in learning more about your rental and the idea of making it their new home when they can see themselves residing there.

Be Genuinely Precise
Tell a tale, but be sure it represents your rental home correctly. Don't embellish the truth about your home by spinning a fairytale! Additionally, make sure the property is properly depicted in your images. When a tenant arrives for a viewing, they want to see the exact same rental property—in the same superb condition—that they have seen on the internet. Don't mislead buyers with your listing if your Detroit investment property needs work to be competitive.

Collaborate with a property manager to implement astute renovations, build an appealing house, and ensure that the listing accurately portrays a house that prospective tenants will adore.

Ensure your Price in the Listing

It's weird that we would have to remind owners of rental properties of this, but don't forget to include the price tag. It's astonishing how many rental listings there are online without the price mentioned. This makes the entire offering ambiguous and maybe unsettling. Never fail to disclose the rental amount. Add the security deposit on the list as well. Your phone calls will decrease as a result of this. Before they set up a showing, tenants will know if you're inside their budget or not.

It is important that you correctly price your rental. To determine how much properties are renting for, do some market research in your area and set a competitive pricing for your own. Make sure your price plan takes into account any additional facilities you may be providing, such as a pool or extra amenities. Before you put a price on your property and offer it in your listing, you should gather reliable data. If no one contacts you to book a viewing, it's possible that your asking price is too high.

Mind the Fair Housing Compliance

A listing can be troublesome if you are not familiar with fair housing regulations. When it comes to renting property, the Fair Housing Act is a significant federal statute, and California's fair housing rules offer even more protections than those found in the federal legislation. Your listing description cannot contain any language that would be interpreted as discriminatory against any of the federal or state-recognized protected classes. Avoid implying that your property is "good" for a specific type of tenant. Don't bring up the fact that it isn't kid-safe. You do not need to specify that your property is near certain places of worship.

Highlight the qualities that everyone would find appealing in your rental home in order to attract as many potential tenants as you can.

Property Advertising Strategy

You can start marketing your listing to locate renters as soon as you've typed out your listing, proofread and spell-checked it, and obtained some current, high-quality photos. It's usually a good idea to market a property listing through a variety of channels in order to optimize its visibility. Posting it on as many free websites as you can before moving on to paid platforms is one way to get started. While premium channels frequently yield higher-quality leads, free channels could yield an equivalent amount of leads.

When it comes to promoting your home, your main goal should be to reach as many relevant and qualified applicants as possible. We look at five different strategies to market your rental property in order to attract tenants.

Word of mouth - The method of finding renters through word-of-mouth could take many forms. Inform the tenants of your other units, for instance, that there is a vacancy coming up. Furthermore, tell your friends and family about the situation; maybe one of them knows someone who is looking for housing. Of course, you should also post it on your personal social media pages, like Facebook. You might even sweeten the deal by providing a little rent relief option or gift card as a form of commission if they locate you as a tenant. Don't be hesitant to take use of traditional social networking.

In fact, you might even make a straightforward, interesting, and shareable movie promoting the property and advantages of living there using an inexpensive video testimonial technique.

Use for rent signs - Although it may seem outdated, posting a for rent sign outside of your building is nevertheless effective. Local traffic and even neighborhood residents who are interested in who lives next door may see these for rent signs. Even while they aren't likely to generate as much interest as some of the other strategies on this list (like online rental listings), the inquiries they do generate will be highly targeted at individuals who are already aware of the advantages of relocating soon and are considering living in that location.

When combined with other rental property promotion tactics, it's an affordable approach to inform people about availability and can generate some quality leads. Furthermore, even if the individual passing the for rent sign isn't in the market for a property, they may know someone who is and direct them to you.

But not everyone needs a for rent sign, and not every place is a good fit for one. In our ever-evolving rental marketing landscape, the following list of benefits and drawbacks of employing for rent signs will help you decide if it's the appropriate move for your rental business.

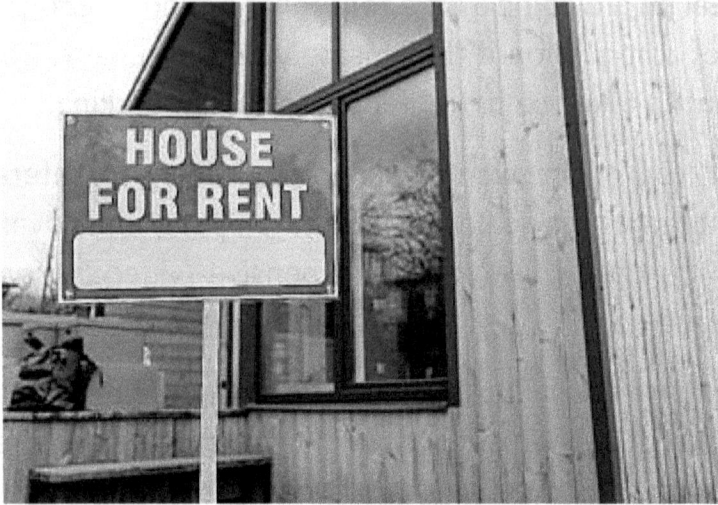

Pros

o *Quantity of inquiries.* Depending on where your home is located, a lot of people will probably notice the for rent sign; if it's in a cul-de-sac, it won't be as effective. Many of those people will either be looking for a rental or know someone who is.

o *The neighbors' assistance.* The residents of the neighborhood have a stake in who resides on their street in your rental property. Therefore, there's a potential that your neighbors will assist you in filling it if they notice the for rent sign; they might even know someone who is looking. Word-of-mouth recommendations frequently produce excellent leads.

- *Price*. Signs are a rather cheap way to attract attention to your home and find new renters if you are renting it out. You may reuse these signs for years to come, and they usually cost $20 or less.

<u>Con</u>
- *Theft*. Properties that are vacant are prime targets for burglars. Putting up a "For Rent" sign might sometimes serve as an advertisement to burglars.
- *Unqualified Leads*. Time lost on unqualified leads can be enormous. If you post your phone number on a sign for rent, many people will take it as an open invitation to contact you, even if they are not actually interested in renting from you.
- *There are more effective advertising methods*. Much of the tenant search process can be automated with the use of contemporary technologies. A "For Rent" sign can draw some attention, but might not be the best approach for you.

Professional Website - Over the past few decades, people's methods for looking for rentals have evolved. People will typically start their search online. Having a quality website and an online presence can be a fantastic strategy to draw tenants to your rental listing. With just one click, you can use Landlord Studio to create a free rental listing and syndicate it to popular rental listing websites like Hotpads, Zumper, Zillow, Craigslist, and Trulia.

Flyers - Flyers may work well for exposing your rental to the right kind of people, depending on where it is located and the local population. This is a rather cheap method of finding tenants and gives you the opportunity to include some good images, a description, and information about how they may get in touch with you. You can make eye-catching flyers at a reasonable cost by using resources like Freepik, a well-known online platform for graphic design.

Open Houses - A rental open house can be a useful approach to generate interest and attract tenants, much like an open house for a for-sale home. Additionally, it saves you from having to schedule several separate viewings with interested parties and enables you to meet potential tenants in person. Awareness is crucial. To boost traffic, ensure that the Open House is posted on several websites. One option to combine methods and make this rental property advertising method successful is to put up a "For Rent" sign on the lawn with information about the open house dates.

Local Newspaper - Although the newspaper industry has undoubtedly evolved over time, the idea of the neighborhood classified section is still very much alive and well. Even while many newspapers have made the switch to online distribution, they continue to list a variety of items, from pets for sale to—you guessed it—rental homes. Look at your neighborhood or local newspaper to find out the requirements for becoming listed.

Attracting the Right Tenants

An investment property is an asset that generates income and can make or break your journey to financial freedom. Beyond just arranging for potential renters to view the property, property management also includes maintenance and lease signing. Prepare to wear several hats if you're a landlord or property manager working alone. We do not mean "jack-of-all-trades; master of none." You have to do everything correctly.

Although property management may seem daunting at first, there are numerous resources and recommendations available to make the process more efficient. This allows you to concentrate on the most crucial aspect of property management, which is selecting and keeping renters of the best possible quality. While you are seeking high-quality tenants, rest assured that they are also looking for high-quality landlords. It's a two-way street, and showing empathy (putting yourself in their situation) is essential for gaining their trust and signing the leasing agreement.

Before diving into checklists for obtaining high-quality renters to your rental property, consider what an ideal tenant means to you. Just as a firm would consider their buyer's persona, what is your tenant's persona? Landlords seek out a variety of attributes in tenants, but the most common mistake they make is copying and pasting them off the internet and expecting the appropriate tenants to fall from the skies and into their properties.

Generally, one may assume that the characteristics of superior tenants consist solely of: Timely rent payment and little to no damages. While this might sound right, they are actually wrong. All of this is their obligation as lessees. In theory, this ought to be the very minimum. If not legally, then it is their responsibility to maintain their temporary residence, pay their rent, and adhere to the terms of their rental agreement.

Here are traits that indicator a high-quality tenant

- Respectful to management and neighbors (e.g., no noise complaints, respect the rules)
- Fair, decent, kind, and logical
- Pay on time and in full, ideally through auto-payment.
- No harm to the apartment after the contract is over
- Refer their friends

One major issue that most landlords and property managers deal with is that tenants sometimes move on before realizing they were the ideal tenant, which leaves them with regrets.

Quiet tenants and early payers who always greet the elderly lady next door may not necessarily look like high-quality tenants. It is only after they have left that you realize just how great they were.

Tenants by Generations
Break down your screening criteria into age, income, job, and your degree of involvement. Why is this the last item on the list, you ask? Because that's how involved you'll need to be, depending on the generation of your prospective tenant.

126

Understanding generational disparities is important since they reflect distinct needs.

Baby boomers and Generation X – These are the least likely generations to rent because most of them were reared with a preference for owning a home. If they do decide to rent, though, they are frequently dependable, high-quality, and low-maintenance tenants.

Millennials – Pioneers in exploring new lifestyles. They'll give up their big suburban single-family house in favor of a compact apartment near their "vibe" locations, which are tech hubs, upscale districts, and urban hotspots.

Older Generation Z, or college students – This group requires the most care. The majority of this generation lives in college towns or cities; therefore, you may have to deal with a greater turnover rate because they are not exactly known for taking good care of their belongings, especially if they don't own them. The key to a successful college rental market is having clear ground rules.

Maintain a neutral stance on your prospective tenant's ethnicity, gender, and disability. Discrimination in housing is prohibited by law for both moral and legal reasons.

There are numerous ways to recruit high-quality renters to your rental property. Nothing, though, can match the conventional word-of-mouth approach. And we don't just mean informing individuals that you have a vacancy. We suggest offering an excellent experience to your tenants so that they will promote you to their family, friends, and coworkers.

<u>Features that attract high quality tenants</u>

The caliber of your tenant is directly proportional to the value you provide. High-quality renters appreciate high-quality amenities, services, and features, such as:

- o *Lease terms* – Is it long-term, short-term or customizable?
- o *Furnished* – Is it fully furnished, partially furnished, or an empty slate?
- o *Utilities* – Are utilities like TV, internet, water, and electricity included? For older generations, especially, setting up TV and internet can be a chore, so this is an easy win.
- o *Appliances* - For residential units, does it include a dryer/washer inside?
- o *Reviews* - The younger generation will conduct as much research on you and your property as you will on them. Make sure you have the best online reviews possible.
- o *References* - When you happen to run across other tenants during the walking tour, do they treat you well? Does it demonstrate to a potential tenant that you have positive relationships with your current tenants?

Trust is the most valuable asset in real estate. People do not conduct business with those they do not trust. Communication, honesty, and transparency are essential.

CHAPTER EIGHT
SCREENING AND SELECTING TENANTS

Finding responsible and trustworthy renters for your rental properties necessitates a thorough tenant screening and selection procedure. Investing time in thoroughly screening applications can help you avoid future issues and guarantee that the best tenants are placed in your home. The tenant selection procedure is critical for landlords seeking dependable, long-term renters. Making educated decisions will be made possible by efficiently conducting property showings, carefully reviewing applications, and carrying out due diligence by checking references and background information.

Establishing Screening Criteria

If you own or manage a property, you must develop a set of standards for screening potential tenants. This will help you not only find excellent tenants but also determine whether they satisfy your minimum rental needs. It reduces the risk of a discrimination claim by allowing property managers or landlords to avoid their own subjective views. Here's how to set the ideal renter screening criteria:

Think of your Primary Objective

To create objective tenant screening criteria, you must first identify your major goals. Your main objectives ought to be:

o Adherence to fair housing standards is essential for mitigating the risk of discrimination claims.

o Ability to personally select the best renters; tenants should be reliable and timely payers of their rent. Also, they ought to abide by lease and rental agreements.

Identify Factors that will aid you in Accomplishing these Goals

In order to successfully create your tenant screening criteria, it would be best to consider a few specific factors. You ought to think about the Fair Housing Bill, for example. The Equitable Housing Act specifies guidelines for property owners regarding how to offer rental applicants equitable housing possibilities.

The bill forbids discrimination based on gender, ethnicity, class, or gender identity. Landlord-tenant laws are another important consideration. In accordance with these rules, it is the duty of property managers and owners to make sure that renters give information about their employment, income, and proof of identity.

Find Suitable Tenants

Find a method to evaluate a potential tenant's suitability for your rental asset. Of course, in your search for the ideal client, you must adhere to the law. For example, you can get information about a tenant's suitability by getting in touch with their previous landlords and asking about their renting history. Another option to help you in your quest is to look for a tenant screening service. Here are a few unbiased, compliant methods to determine if a potential tenant is worth renting your property:

- Verify whether the applicant's monthly income is three times more than their monthly rent.
- Take into account the candidate's monthly salary and debt-to-income ratio to make sure they won't struggle to pay the rent.
- Examine the applicant's credit history to determine their level of financial responsibility.
- Examine the applicant's history of making on-time rent payments.
- Find out whether the applicant has a history of being evicted for failing to pay rent.
- Determine if the candidate has a reliable source of income.

Evaluate Applicants adherence to Terms and Conditions

This step is vital in developing effective tenant screening criteria. Determine whether each applicant can follow the terms and conditions of the rental. Your assessment should not be based on personal opinion. The following are some objective and legal methods to evaluate an applicant's propensity to abide by the terms and conditions of the rental:

- Verify if the applicant has ever been convicted of a crime for previous offenses.

- Find out from previous landlords if the potential tenant has a history of noise complaints.
- Verify if the applicant has ever violated a lease before.
- Verify whether the applicant has ever been evicted for violating a lease.
- Ensure that the applicant does not fabricate any application information.

Put it Together

Before you begin taking rental applications from potential tenants, compile your list of requirements for the tenant screening process. Bring your evaluation to a lawyer. Real estate laws, particularly those pertaining to landlord-tenant situations, should be familiar to the lawyer. This is a crucial step because it guarantees that your tenant screening standards will abide by local, state, and federal housing laws. After an attorney reviews the application materials, apply your standards progressively and uniformly to each candidate. Follow your tenant screening requirements to the letter. Don't give in to any exceptions. Above all, speak in a language that is easy for everyone to understand. Steer clear of jargon and complicated legal words. Plain and straightforward language ensures that the applicant understands all aspects of the tenant screening process.

All in all, tenant screening criteria are essential for every property manager and landlord. Make sure your requirements take into account the interests of both you and your potential tenants.

Conducting Tenant Background Check

Before signing a rental agreement, prospective tenants are often subjected to a background check. When a renter applies for a rental, landlords and property managers employ profess-ional background screening agencies to verify the applicant's credit, rental history, eviction history, and criminal record. Landlords can discover trustworthy and reputable tenants who are likely to pay rent on time, take care of the property, and abide by the terms of the lease by doing a thorough background check on prospective tenants.

A typical tenant background check involves several steps:

- *Get written consent* – Written tenant consent is required before proceeding with a background check. According to the Fair Credit Reporting Act, access to a consumer's personal information is prohibited unless it is needed for "permissible purposes," such as housing. This might be a separate form or a component of the rental application.
- *Gather the necessary information* - Having a thorough rental application is the first important step. It should include the following information: name, date of birth, Social Security number, information about other potential occupants, pets, past addresses with landlord references, employment references, information about the vehicle, and a driver's license or other official identification. A copy of the applicant's ID, as well as

proof of income, such as bank statements, pay stubs, or a W-2, are required.

The quality of the information entered determines how well a background check turns out. Additionally, the likelihood of a renter forging documents decreases with the amount of documentation that a landlord demands.

- *Credit check* – If the tenant screening provider does not provide a credit check, landlords can obtain a credit report from Equifax, TransUnion, and Experian, the three main credit reporting agencies. The applicant's utility bills, overdue rent, payday loans, and any recent late payments on their credit lines are among the information that can be found on their credit report, even if it won't tell you everything. Credit reports no longer include information about tax liens or civil judgments, which includes evictions. "Unless the tenant is taken to court and a collection agency is used to collect the verdict, there will be no effect on their credit.

- Employment history – The employment history of the tenant is a crucial consideration when analyzing the results of their background check. Employment gaps could indicate that a tenant is unable to maintain employment or generate a steady income in another way. You should get in touch with an applicant's prior employers if you have any reason to believe they have lied about how long they have worked at a company or created a false resume. Background checks provide at least the company's contact information, including its phone number, email address, and physical address. It's possible that the company a tenant claims to have worked for doesn't exist if this fundamental contact information is missing.

- *Check references* – Always be sure to verify references, and if you'd rather not handle it yourself, you can engage a company to do it on your behalf. Anyone can forge a pay stub and avoid having their landlord bring them before the court. Speak with their employer's HR department directly and the previous landlord to get the truth, which isn't officially included in the "public record" that is provided for a credit and background check. It may appear overwhelming, but bad tenants hope landlords won't get into trouble.

- *Know the local laws* – The rights and obligations of both parties in a landlord-tenant relationship are outlined by specific legislation. Landlords who are ignorant of tenant laws run the risk of inadvertently violating the rights of their tenants or failing to uphold their own legal commitments. Discrimination is prohibited by Fair Housing legislation, such as asking someone not to apply based on their criminal history. Additionally, in the event that the applicant fails the background check, the landlord has a legal duty to notify the applicant of the action, include the contact details of the organization that provided the report, and specify the applicant's right to have any erroneous information corrected and a free copy of the report sent to them within sixty days of the landlord's decision.

Special Considerations

Finding the ideal tenant for each of your properties can be a difficult one. To prevent vacancies, you'll probably need to make some compromises on your rental criteria; the parameters you decide to give up on are entirely your choice. An applicant with a clean criminal record or one without a rental history but with a respectable credit score are both viable candidates for your rental property. Sometimes, though, it's better to avoid taking the chance. Candidates with violent criminal histories or those who are registered sex offenders may pose an excessive risk to your rental property. It may also be decided that a tenant is too risky if they have already been caught committing crimes at another apart-ment.

Both your interests as a property owner and the safety of the existing renters must be considered when choosing an applicant for approval, as they are in this instance intert-wined. You wouldn't want to rent to the incorrect tenant and endanger your apartment or your tenants.

In summary, the most crucial thing to remember when running a background check on a tenant is to assess their rental, criminal, job, and credit histories using the report. Additional tenant information, such as racial origin, sexual orientation, and familial status, should not be utilized to reject or reduce a renter's chances of approval, as this is deemed discriminatory and illegal. Prior to conducting background checks on applicants, you must also get their signed consent. As usual, make sure you're following the rules when it comes to tenant screening to ensure that you're not creating any miscommunications with potential tenants.

Attracting Quality Tenants

Attracting good tenants is crucial for a landlord to keep a profitable and stress-free commercial property. A quality tenant will take responsibility for the property, pay rent on time, and maintain it on its own. On the other hand, problematic tenants may result in headaches, financial losses, or even legal issues. Consequently, it's essential to implement suitable strategies in order to land quality tenants. Here are eight ways to attract quality tenants.

Effective Advertisement: Effective property advertisement is one vital part of attracting quality tenants. Ads should be readable, informative, and visually appealing. It should contain information on the property's location, features, size, and amenities. Select the best images and videos to showcase the property's features. Additionally, be sure to advertise your property on a variety of platforms, including rental websites, local newspapers, and social media.

Set the Right Price: Setting the correct price for your rental property is critical for attracting quality tenants. A high rent may prevent you from landing quality tenants, and a low rent may entice irresponsible or financially unstable tenants. Investigate the local rental market and take into account the size, location, features, and amenities of the property in order to determine the appropriate price.

Property Maintenance: Property maintenance is essential for attracting quality tenants. Ensure that the property is in good condition, well-maintained, and clean. If necessary, replace any broken appliances, fix any damage, and paint the walls. Additionally, ensure that the exterior of the property is attractive and that the landscaping is in good shape.

Offer Amenities: Providing amenities can draw better tenants and raise the property's worth. A laundry room, a parking garage, a fitness center, and a swimming pool are a few of the famous amenities. Make sure, though, that the amenities you offer fit both your budget and target market.

Screen Tenants Thoroughly: To attract quality tenants, tenants must be screened thoroughly. Conduct a background, credit, and rental history check on every applicant. Additionally, confirm their income and employment to ensure that they are capable of paying the rent. Furthermore, to confirm that they were accountable tenants, ask for references from prior landlords.

Provide Excellent Customer Service: Improving customer service can help attract quality tenants and improve tenant retention. Respond quickly to their complaints, inquiries, and repair requests. Additionally, communicate with them in a clear and concise manner and treat them with professionalism and respect.

Offer Lease Incentives: Providing lease incentives has the potential to draw in high-caliber tenants and boost tenant retention. Popular lease incentives consist of a gift card, a free month's rent, or a discount on their first month's rent. Nevertheless, be sure to provide incentives that align with your target market and budget.

Partner with Local Businesses: Forming partnerships with local companies can help attract quality tenants and improve tenant satisfaction. For instance, provide tenants with discounts at local stores, restaurants, or gyms. This has the potential to enhance the property's appeal to prospective tenants and boost tenant retention.

Emphasize Safety and Security: A strong emphasis on security and safety can draw better tenants and boost tenant retention. Ensure that the property has smoke detectors, secure locks, and adequate lighting. Additionally, install a security system and give the tenants emergency contact details. Putting a strong emphasis on security and safety can draw in more potential tenants and raise tenant satisfaction levels.

Create a pet-friendly Environment: Environments that are pet-friendly can help attract quality tenants and improve tenant retention. A lot of tenants are pet owners and are willing to pay more for a home that allows pets. Think about allowing pets in exchange for a pet rent or pet deposit. Additionally, offer pet-friendly amenities like a grooming station or a dog park.

By employing these strategies, landlords may attract quality tenants, improve tenant retention, and sustain a successful rental investment.

CHAPTER NINE
MANAGING TENANCIES EFFECTIVELY

When you become a landlord, the most crucial thing is to make sure you have decent tenants. Renters are the lifeblood of your business, but finding and maintaining tenants may be challenging, particularly if you own a large number of rental properties. Basically, tenant management means keeping your tenants organized, handling their rent payments, maintaining the property, and maintaining records with all the pertinent data. Ensuring seamless operations between you and the occupants of your property is the main goal.

Establishing Clear Communication Channels

Maintaining a great connection and a well-run property as a property owner/manager depends on having effective communication with your tenants. Tenants want assurance that their property owners/managers are approachable, open, and considerate—whether they have a straightforward inquiry about rent or a more complicated maintenance concern. Even so, there are still a lot of obstacles that property

managers must overcome in order to have effective communications with their renters.

Thus, in the following sections, we'll examine some of the
typical difficulties faced by property managers and offer
advice and techniques for enhancing tenant communication.
By doing this, you ought to be able to forge closer bonds with
your tenants and make sure that everyone has a more positive
and successful renting experience.

Understand your Tenants
To effectively interact with your tenants, you must first learn
their specific wants and preferences regarding the rental
property. Each tenant has a unique communication style and
set of channels that they choose to use. You may better satisfy
the wants and expectations of your tenants by taking the time
to get to know them and to customize your communication
techniques. The following are some recommendations for
understanding your tenants:

- o *Understanding your tenants' requirements and communication preferences*: Not all tenants communicate in
  the same manner or have the same wants. While some
  tenants might prefer text messages, emails, or first-
  class certified mail, others would prefer phone calls. It's
  crucial to understand these preferences in order to
  guarantee effective communication.
- o *Tenant feedback surveys*: Tenant feedback on communication preferences, satisfaction with present communication techniques, and areas for development can
  all be obtained through surveys. This can be accom-

plished through the use of online survey tools, email surveys delivered to their mailing address, or hardcopy surveys.

o *Frequent tenant check-ins*: Property managers can benefit from periodically learning about the requirements and preferences of their occupants. These check-ins can be done via email, phone, or in person. Check-ins, for instance, may take place following the completion of maintenance requests or following the conclusion of an event hosted on site.

o *Multiple communication channels*: It's possible that tenants would rather interact via various means. You can make sure that tenants may contact you in a method that suits them best by offering a variety of channels for communication, including email, text messaging, and phone calls.

Understanding the demands and communication preferences of your renters can help you develop a communication strategy that will suit their needs, as well as make sure your message is understood.

Consistent and Clear Message

A clear and consistent message is also necessary for effective property management communication. If you want to understand how to interact with renters as a property manager, you must first ensure that your words are received and understood. This can be accomplished by tailoring your messages to match your tenants' specific needs. Adding images and visuals to written words can be a powerful strategy. They can make complex material more understandable and visually appealing.

For example, an infographic might assist in explaining a new policy or providing step-by-step directions for a specific process, such as maintenance requests. This can be very helpful for renters who might have trouble writing or who don't speak the same language. Ensuring tenants receive printed papers in their native tongue is another smart way to guarantee consistent and clear communication. Tenants may find it easier to understand messages and feel more at ease speaking with their property manager if materials are provided in their mother tongue.

This will promote effective communication between landlords and tenants, regardless of language barriers, and can be particularly significant if the tenant population at the property is diverse. Property managers should ensure that all messaging is consistent with the property's brand and objective. This means that all communications have to align with the property's reputation, values, and objectives. For example, if the property is committed to sustainability, its messaging should stress sustainability programs and goals. This strengthens the property's brand, fosters trust, and attracts more potential tenants.

Responsive and Timely Communication
Maintaining a strong tenant relationship requires timely and responsive communication. In order to gain tenants' trust and show that their complaints are being taken seriously, it is imperative for property managers to swiftly address any

correspondence they receive. One of the most critical parts of timely and responsive communication is to establish clear reaction timings. Tenants should be informed about how long they should anticipate to wait for a response to a scheduled repair or any other contact endeavor.

The property's email signature, website, and automated social media messaging can all be used to pass on this information. Making use of property management software, can also facilitate appropriate communication management and guarantee prompt response times to messages.

Property management software can assist automate resp-onses to typical questions and send out notifications when messages arrive. This can assist property managers in main-taining contact with tenants even during busy times. It's also critical to respond quickly to complaints and problems from tenants. This helps to address any issues before they worsen and demonstrates to tenants that their demands are being taken seriously. To encourage excellent communication skills, you should let tenants know how to get in touch with you in an emergency and address pressing concerns as soon as possible.

Empathy and Understanding
Understanding and empathy are essential elements of a successful tenant communication strategy. When addressing issues, like extending the rent payment period, you should actively listen to the concerns of the tenants and demonstrate empathy. This can improve communication and foster a sense of trust between the renters and the property owner/

manager. A vital ability for any property manager is active listening. It entails paying close attention to the tenant and making an effort to comprehend their viewpoint.

Property managers should listen to tenants' problems without interrupting, stay involved, and follow up with questions to get clarification. This demonstrates that the property manager respects the tenant's viewpoint and is dedicated to coming up with a workable solution. Effective communication also requires the ability to empathize with and understand others.

Property managers ought to show that they are aware of the tenant's worries and how the problem is affecting them. Tenants may have a better interaction with the property manager as a result of feeling heard and validated. It's crucial to keep in mind that tenants could have a range of unique requirements, experiences, and viewpoints. By being empathetic and understanding, you can foster a closer bond with them.

And finally, providing options and solutions to tenants' demands might show that a property manager is dedicated to finding a solution for any problems that may arise. Property managers ought to outline their plans for resolving the problem, including a schedule for doing so and any necessary next steps.

Build that Landlord-Tenant Relationship
Effective communication, efficient property management, and profitable property ownership all depend on developing

strong relationships with tenants. Renters are more inclined to extend their leases and refer new tenants to the property if they have a strong sense of belonging with both the manager and the property. Building trusting connections with tenants requires establishing a warm, inclusive atmosphere. This can be accomplished through giving tenants a feeling of community and cultivating a positive sense of belonging.

Keeping the common areas tidy, secure, and well-maintained is one-way property managers may foster a friendly atmosphere. Property managers can also try to interact with tenants by showing up in a polite and personable manner. Putting together events and activities for renters can also promote a sense of community and strengthen bonds between them.

You can encourage tenants to connect and get to know one another by hosting events like barbecues, holiday parties, or game evenings. Tenants may feel more a part of their property and have a good sense of community as a result. Building good relationships with tenants also requires giving them the opportunity to provide input and comments. Online forums, suggestion boxes, and recurring surveys can all be used for that. By requesting feedback from various renters, property managers can find areas for improvement while also demonstrating their dedication to fulfilling tenant demands.

Effective tenant communication is essential to managing rental properties well. Building good connections with tenants, raising tenant satisfaction and retention rates can all be achieved with clear, consistent, timely, and empathic communication. Implementing the tactics outlined above will allow you to improve communication with your tenants, increase tenant happiness, and ultimately drive success for your properties.

Handling Maintenance Requests

If you are a property manager or owner, you understand how important upkeep and repairs are. When problems emerge in rental units, it is critical to address them quickly to maintain tenant protection, satisfaction, and convenience. As a landlord, you must keep your rental properties in good condition and handle repair requests quickly. This not only keeps your tenants satisfied and your homes in good condition, but it also protects your investment in the long run.

Maintenance requests are one of the biggest headaches for landlords when a vacancy is filled. Not only is it difficult to organize schedules between renters and maintenance people, but repairs can have a negative impact on both your personal and professional lives.

Being a landlord is a full-time job; for example, if a tenant calls at midnight reporting flooding in their apartment, you have to answer, try to arrange a repair through negotiation, work with the renter, and then try to get someone to come out and solve the problem. Not only is your private life disrupted, but a repair that is not handled efficiently and promptly is also costly to your business.

Managing Expectations with your Tenants

Without a doubt, controlling tenants' expectations is a critical component of managing maintenance. The landlord-tenant relationship may become very tense due to maintenance. Whatever maintenance schedule you decide on for your rental property, make sure the tenant is aware of it so that expectations are set right away. Similar to maintenance, being proactive is preferable to being reactive. The manner in which you and your tenants handle repairs for your rentals now will determine how your landlord-tenant relationship develops later on and how future property maintenance issues are resolved. This is something that your lease can (and should) specifically state. Here are some suggestions on what to include:

Outline property maintenance policies – If you have any policies about the upkeep of the property, ensure that your lease specifies and defines them precisely. Here are some questions to think about when you prepare rental property maintenance lease addenda, if you haven't already:

- When a tenant needs repairs, who should they call?
- For maintenance, how can a tenant get in touch with you or others?
- What is the process for requesting emergency maintenance?
- What upkeep is the tenant's responsibility for?

Recall that every state has regulations pertaining to maintenance, repairs, and upkeep between landlords and tenants.

As such, it's critical that you understand how these obligations connect to your lease maintenance policy.

Layout tenant's responsibility – When it comes to maintaining your rental property in good condition, you should explicitly state in your lease what maintenance the tenant is accountable for. You should create an inspection schedule and explicitly define what repairs your tenants are liable for. A survey found that 78% of all rental repair concerns are normally covered by landlords. The breakdown of these difficulties is as follows:

Percentage of Specific Repairs Covered by Landlords	
Repair a broken major appliance (e.g., stove, fridge)	86.8%
Repair broken windows	86.1%
Repair broken toilets	84.5%
Solve drain issues	77.5%
Change air filters	48.5%
Change lightbulbs	13.0%

Set up regular routine inspections of the rental – Regardless of how excellent a tenant they are, you should still set up an inspection plan and procedure to make sure they are maintaining your home. It's easy to overlook or put off preventative property care, so keeping up with it is critical to protecting your investment. Additionally, maintaining a well-kept and inspected property will keep tenants satisfied. Although the schedule needs to be specified in the lease, it's crucial to do routine rental inspections to make sure your tenants are doing their part. This preventative maintenance guarantees that greater concerns (broken heaters, fire dangers, etc.) do not build up as a result of neglect.

Ensuring Maintenance Requests are Received

Maintenance issues are likely to arise at around 2 p.m. on Mondays or at midnight on Fridays. We advise you to have a plan in place for handling the situation before it arises, to ensure that you can get notifications, and to know how you will be informed.

Provide contact information – Landlords frequently maintain two separate contact lists: personal and business. It will be up to you what information about your contact details you decide to include. We advise, however, that you create business-related professional contact details exclusively. In the unlikely event that you need to evict a renter, having a business phone number and email address puts up a barrier between you and your tenants that prevents the disclosure of your personal contact details.

Layout effective channels of communication – It's important to choose your preferred methods of getting in touch with tenants. It is up to you to select whether business-oriented contact information works best for the business and your comfort level. Establishing the most effective method of communication, whether it be through text, email, or phone call, is equally crucial. Also, if you choose premium maintenance services, inform the tenant that they will be the first point of contact for repair issues. The following are recommendations for creating communication channel best practices:

- o *Text/Phone*: If you don't receive messages after missing calls, check your voicemail. Also, make sure you have the tenant's number saved. Avoid being the person whose voicemail is overflowing when your tenant's flat leaks! If texting is comfortable for you, let your tenant know that it is OK.
- o *Email*: Enable notifications for the specified email address. Perhaps design one specifically for the property, or make sure to include your tenants' email information as well.
- o *Online Maintenance Request Form*: When you join your renters to online maintenance, such as RentRedi, they will be able to make maintenance requests right from their app. This gives you a uniform form for collecting data, which you can use to handle requests more quickly and determine the exact level of severity—or lack thereof—of the problem directly from your RentRedi maintenance dashboard. You will be notified through the RentRedi app whenever a new maintenance request is made.
- o *Premium Maintenance Services*: In the event that you utilize online premium maintenance services, i.e Rent-Redi, make sure the renter has saved the dedicated

phone number (which is featured in the online app and supplied in the welcome email) so they will be contacting them rather than you. Contractors and tenants can handle problems on their own, and you can monitor and control everything from the online maintenance dashboard.

Using the maintenance request form – In order to create effective channels of communication for maintenance requests, it is important to understand the problem. Tenants sometimes find it difficult to explain the exact nature of a problem over email or text, so developing a form that can gather consistent data, classify the problem, and even attach images can be quite helpful in deciphering maintenance difficulties. Property management software, such as Rent-Redi, is an effective way to properly handle maintenance requests via renter mobile apps.

In order for landlords to see exactly what is happening, tenants can submit a description of the issue, categorize it (such as electricity, water, heat/AC, etc.), write any remarks, and then attach a 5-second video showing the maintenance problem.

Building a Maintenance Team
Maintenance related to HVAC, plumbing, electricity, general handyman repairs, and yard or landscape upkeep are some of the more frequent maintenance issues. Having people & connections for every typical problem is essential to being proactive & organized when it comes to maintaining rental properties. There are several strategies to begin creating a

maintenance team and expanding your maintenance network if you're just getting started in rental property management.

Review sites and research – You can look for rental property maintenance service providers on a number of websites that rank and review service providers. Depending on the site you choose, you can see how others rate a service provider and whether or not they have been background checked and screened. Examples of these are HomeAdvisor, Yelp, BBB.

Online/local landlord forums – Asking around can help you construct a list. If you are not a member of any local groups, there are several social networking sites that can help you identify and connect with real estate professionals and land-lords in your region. Examples are Facebook Groups, Word of Mouth, Meetup, Reddit, BiggerPockets. These groups can offer insider knowledge on which maintenance professionals in your area are the finest to choose for repairs.

Vetted maintenance service contractors – Premium main-tenance services are an excellent substitute if you've run out of choices for research, are unable to locate the ideal maintenance expert match, or cannot currently afford a full-time maintenance crew. With online premium maintenance services, you can access a network of well-regarded, comp-etent maintenance contractors who can effectively manage all repairs, including emergency ones, without having to pay for a full-time maintenance expert.

Manage Maintenance Timely

Haven included maintenance rental property policies, established efficient channels of communication, and arranged a maintenance team. It is important to make sure you handle maintenance requests timely. If you are doing your own maintenance, it is essential that you reply rapidly to requests. This legally means within 24 to 48 hours in several states.

While policies like landlords and renter's insurance might assist in paying for property damages in the event of a major problem, insurance companies may need documentation of the problem, the solution, and the issue. Importantly, responding swiftly to requests is the best way to avoid damaging your property. Renter repairs can be promptly resolved and your property investment safeguarded if you have premium maintenance. Receipts and tracking data are required for tax purposes as well as to ensure that all repairs are documented.

Relocating Tenants for Repairs

Tenants are assumed to stay at the property for a set amount of time under a lease agreement. However, in some cases, it is not feasible to make renters remain on the premises and pay rent if the damage to the property is severe enough. Even though the agreement is still in force, the renters might need to leave the rental property for a period of time. A landlord may have to relocate their tenants in an emergency in order to keep them safe. For instance, you could have to provide a renter with additional suitable lodging or temporarily move them to a different apartment if the rental unit:

- Suffers from intense cold or heat

- Contains potentially fatal elements like radiation or mold.
- Is condemned by health officials
- There are other issues that prevent it from even being substantially inhabited

As you can see, you have a lot of alternatives when it comes to maintaining your rental property. Having a system in place for overseeing maintenance is essential for safeguarding your investment in real estate, preserving good relations between landlord and tenant, and cutting expenses related to rental upkeep.

Dealing with Late Payments and Evictions

Ensuring regular rental payments is critical for maintaining a stable cash flow, but handling late-paying tenants can be difficult for landlords. Before taking severe action against tenants who have not made their rent payments, think about using these tactics to settle the matter amicably and legally.

Proactive Measures

Clarify Lease Conditions: To prevent misunderstandings, make sure the lease agreement makes clear the conditions of payment, the dates on which they are due, and the repercussions of making late payments. Make sure the lease is signed and initialed by every adult renter residing on the property to attest to their understanding of its provisions.

Conduct Thorough Screening on Tenants: Before finalizing a lease agreement, undertake a thorough tenant screening to reduce the chance of late payments. Credit reports, employment certifications, and references from prior renters should all be part of this.

Use Online Payment Choices: Provide online payment choices to expedite the rent collection procedure. Giving tenants an easy and safe way to pay their rent can help prevent late and missed payments.

Reactive Measures
Maintain Communication: Get in touch with tenants to find out why they missed a payment. A quick reminder via phone or email can help keep the tenant from cultivating bad habits.

Issue a Late Payment Notice: If a renter's late payment results in fees, consider passing these on to the tenant. A reminder of the conditions of the lease and the repercussions of making late payments is sent out via a notice of late rent.

Prepare to take legal action: You might have to think about eviction if your payments are consistently late or unsuccessful. Seek advice from a legal expert to ensure compliance with local laws, as this procedure can be time-consuming and costly.

Encouraging Timely Payments
Provide Flexible Payment Plans: Allowing tenants to make rent payments on a temporary basis while guaranteeing your income during this time will assist tenants facing financial challenges.

<u>Establish a Reward Structure</u>: If a renter routinely pays their rent on time, you might want to think about setting up a reward system. This could be in the form of gift cards, rent savings, or other benefits.

While eviction may be unavoidable in some situations, open communication is essential for healthy landlord-tenant relationships. Working with tenants who are having financial difficulties is typically more cost-effective than evicting and preparing the property for new tenants, which can be costly and time consuming.

Issuing Eviction

An eviction letter is an official letter from a property owner (landlord) to a tenant stating that he or she must follow the terms of the rental agreement or vacate the property. An eviction notice may also be referred to as a 'notice to vacate' or 'quit notice'. The notice is issued when the tenant and the landlord fail to reach an agreement.

The eviction notice may be unconditional or conditional in certain circumstances. If the notice is conditional, it is due to a break in the lease that can be fixed if the renter complies by the deadline. A conditional notice, on the other hand, requires the tenant to vacate the property before the agreed upon date, as there is nothing the tenant can do to stop the eviction.

There are risks associated with writing an eviction notice. Knowing what to include, where to begin, and how to deliver the notice properly can be confusing. Importantly, please refer to your lease, state regulations, and your legal counsel before serving an eviction notice.

There are various reasons why you may need to start writing an eviction notice, including when renters fail to pay rent, violate the contract, damage the property, annoy other tenants, or use the property for illegal purposes. Prior to drafting a tenant eviction notice, carefully review both your state's regulations and your agreement. Importantly, provide the appropriate amount of notice for an eviction. If your lease requires rent to be paid by a specific date, they will be considered to be in breach of contract. Typically, if you have a lease, you can evict a tenant for nonpayment of rent.

After verifying that the tenant should be evicted on clear grounds, issuing an eviction letter is the appropriate next step. Consequently, it is imperative that your letter adhere to both state and local laws and be as formal as possible. The eviction notice is proof that the renter was informed prior to any additional actions being taken. It's essential that you eliminate every possibility of misunderstanding, so be concise, clear, and specific. Once you've acquired all of your papers, it's time to draft a proper eviction notice.

NOTICE TO VACATE

DATE: _____

TENANT: _____

ADDRESS: _____ APT. NO: _____

CITY, STATE, ZIPCODE: _____

Dear TENANT NAME,

You are hereby notified to vacate the premises at _____ by_____.

The reason for giving this notice is as follows:

_____

_____

_____

_____

As stated in the lease, these violations are grounds for eviction. You are hereby notified to vacate and your failure to do so by _____ will force me to initiate eviction proceedings in accordance with the state law.

Thank you in advance for your cooperation.

LANDLORD NAME: _____

SIGNED: _____

DATE: _____

All of your efforts in writing a proper eviction notice will be in vain if the notice is not served to the correct individual. Giving it to the renter in person or to any family member who is older than 18 is the best course of action. You can also deliver the notice via email or by posting it on the tenant's door, as is traditional in some regions.

CHAPTER TEN
RENTAL PROPERTY FOR AIRBNB

A Quick Overview

According to Airbnb data, there are over 4 million hosts globally. There are listings on Airbnb in 100,000 cities worldwide, and the service has more than 150 million users who have made over 1 billion reservations. In North America, an Airbnb typically costs $163 per night. Given these figures, it's easy to see why launching an Airbnb business would seem like a great idea. An Airbnb rental is a short-term vacation rental that several guests book and stay in throughout the year. Apart from Airbnb, properties can also be advertised on other websites for vacation rentals, like FlipKey, HomeToGo, Vrbo, and Homestay.com.

What makes a vacation rental investment such as an Airbnb property a good investment is the popularity of Airbnb itself. Listing a property on the site is regarded as one of the most profitable techniques for real estate investors due to the huge demand for holiday homes and the higher nightly rents that popular tourism locations may fetch. Although the majority of Airbnb hosts begin by leasing a room in a home or utilizing the money from holiday rentals as a side gig, many are able to increase both the size of their portfolio and their revenue, particularly if they buy in popular tourist locations.

Airbnb bookings, like those of many other travel businesses, fell sharply in the early days of the epidemic in 2020. But as travel became more accessible, users swiftly went back to the platform and began scheduling vacations in rural areas far from the crowd. The platform has witnessed a high number of bookings in both rural and urban locations, indicating that the tendency toward remote lodgings is still prevalent.

The profitability of your Airbnb real estate investment will be determined by a few important characteristics, the majority of which have nothing to do with the quality of the property itself. These include the location, annual visitors to the city or town, and real estate market data for the town or city in question.

Airbnb Rental vs Conventional Properties

The distinction between an Airbnb and a traditional rental property boils down to short-term rentals vs long-term tenants. Conventional rental homes offer more stability, consistent cash flow, and a higher occupancy rate than Airbnbs, even though the latter can be more profitable in certain markets due to their higher daily fees. Whether you choose to rent out your house through a traditional long-term lease or as an Airbnb rental has advantages and disadvantages, but ultimately comes down to the following:

The target market: Who is most likely to want to reside in this home? Your decision may be influenced by the location and accessibility of facilities. Short-term guests are more likely to be drawn to a beachfront residence in a popular destination. In contrast, families seeking long-term rentals are more likely to target a house in a safe community near schools and transportation hubs.

Your involvement: Due to the volume of tenants that come through the doors, an Airbnb property will need you to be more involved on a daily basis. To guarantee a steady stream of rental income, you will need to monitor reservations, make sure the house is inspected and cleaned after every tenant vacates, and continue to market the property online.

Your financial goals: While the income from an Airbnb is higher, it is not steady. A typical property, on the other hand, is probably going to provide a more consistent but lesser cash flow. Assume you want to make the most money possible and don't mind getting your hands dirty in the daily management of the property. In that situation, Airbnb is probably your best option because it allows you to significantly enhance your profit margin during peak seasons.

Pros and Cons of Airbnb Rental Property

While there are numerous benefits to having a vacation rental, there are also some drawbacks to Airbnb investment properties. Here are some things to consider when owning an Airbnb rental property:

Pros

- o _Cash flow_: For a well-furnished property in an ideal location, the cash flow and passive income from an Airbnb can be significantly more than the monthly rent from a long-term tenant, sometimes by up to three times more.
- o _Lower maintenance costs_: Depending on how often your visitors check out, you will need to clean the home two or three times a week when using Airbnb. However, you may persuade your tenants to cover the expense of cleaning by adding a $75–$200 cleaning fee

to the nightly rate on Airbnb. Additionally, you have damage coverage for hosts worth up to $1 million.

○ *Flexibility*: When you and a tenant sign a long-term lease, you commit to each other for a minimum of six months and occasionally much longer. However, renting out your house on Airbnb gives you more flexibility. You can use it whenever you want, keep it off the market if you change your mind, or take it down if the earnings aren't what you had hoped for.

○ *Renting the full house is not necessary*: It is possible to use a section of your principal property as a short-term rental property, unlike long-term tenants. You have the option of renting out just one bedroom on Airbnb or part of the house apart from your own living space.

○ *Easy to rent out*: It is usually easier to locate renters for your short-term rental business, even if this will vary depending on your area. This is especially true since advertising your property on Airbnb is the easiest and most affordable option.

Cons

○ *Higher initial costs*: An Airbnb must be tidy, tastefully decorated, and a destination where people would want to spend their vacation in order to consistently book out. This implies that you'll need to invest some time, money, and effort into making sure your Airbnb looks friendly and is competitive with other options on the market, unlike a long-term rental that may be outfitted affordably and rented unfurnished. Moreover, larger down payments may be needed for vacation rental properties.

o *Time-consuming*: Keeping an Airbnb property under management might take a lot of time. For new investors, it's a second job. To operate a successful Airbnb, you need strong managerial and organizational abilityies. After you own a few homes, you can spend money on programs and devices like Lodgify to assist with bookkeeping and money management.

o *Greater risk*: Based on statistical analysis, an increase in the number of visitors staying on your property increases the likelihood of damage and accidents occurring. While you would be screening long-term tenants in your house, it is not practicable to conduct the same background checks on transient visitors.

Investing in Airbnb

After weighing all the pros and cons, you've determined that investing in Airbnb is right for you. There could be a successful career ahead. Now, to begin investing in real estate through Airbnb, here are steps to observe:

Decide the type of property and a budget
Finding out what kind of budget you're working with—that is, how much you can borrow and at what interest rates—will be the first step in this process. Apart from your monthly mortgage payments, you should also account for inspection fees, closing charges, remodeling and maintenance expenses,

and management costs—particularly if you are employing a property management company to handle your hosting.

Identifying the best locations

Finding a profitable market for an Airbnb investment demands:

- Being able to do research on short term renters (STRs)
- Recognizing the STR laws in the markets you want to target

Even if everything else is equal, you can ultimately choose to invest in one market over another because some are more STR-friendly than others. Regulations regarding STR are more lenient in some cities than in others.

For instance, the number of STRs that are actively listed on the Hawaiian island of Maui is severely limited by the local government. Though it may not seem like it, this could actually be a turnoff for investors. With little competition, strong demand, and poor availability, investors who are successful in obtaining a licensed STR on Maui are in a highly advantageous position.

Make sure you investigate each market to find out about any unique zoning rules, taxes, or occupancy limits that can affect your profitability, in addition to any regulations that may apply. However, understanding STR market research needs more than simply legal knowledge. You may also determine if an investment will be as profitable as you anticipate by looking at several metrics that are unique to STRs. Capitalization rates and other statistics can show you how risky an investment is as well as how much money you could make. Knowing these numbers will enable you to identify a good investment opportunity.

Remember that you can get valuable insights into the Airbnb investing landscape by working with a real estate agent who is STR-friendly and has extensive experience in the STR sector.

Analyze Airbnb Market

Before purchasing a property, you must first understand the holiday rental real estate market. While this applies to any real estate transaction, it is especially true for an Airbnb business, since the seasonal rental market can determine whether or not you make a profit on a yearly basis. At this point, it's critical to select the appropriate kind of property: if you're buying in a city, you're probably going to buy a small apartment or condo, as opposed to a resort area, where single-family or multifamily homes typically sell higher. You might also want to think about who is most likely to stay on your property: are you aiming to attract business or family vacationers?

To determine the possible return on investment for your property, make sure to perform a comparative market analysis or consult with a real estate agent. It is important to ascertain the target properties' cap rate and cash-on-cash return.

Seasonality: Almost every market has peak and low seasons, and this is especially true for vacation markets such as lakeside getaways, ski resorts, and beach communities.

Examine the RevPAR on a daily and monthly basis (revenue per available rental, derived by dividing total revenue by number of listings). These indicators can provide historical travel trends, booking windows, and an estimate of revenue growth for each month of the year. Recall: It's important to include the seasonality of your market in your pricing plan.

Short-term rental research: While there is an abundance of vacation rentals in certain markets, there are still undiscovered gems with high occupancy rates. To determine which property types will fit your portfolio and the competitors in your area, you can compare the number of active listings with quarterly rental increases, annual income trends, occupancy rates per city, and types of amenities.

Estimate your investment income
Finding rentals for sale is as easy as deciding on your target market and the size of your home. A good place to start your search for properties that meet your requirements is Zillow. Go through the listings first, then refine your search based on your budget and ideal home features. Make a note of any interesting addresses. Then, based on variables like property type, location, and demand patterns, estimate your income using the AirDNA app. Follow these steps:

- o Enter the addresses of your properties in AirDNA to see rental possibilities.
- o Examine the revenue possibilities in relation to comp-arable local listings.
- o Think about changes in demand and price with the seasons.

o Calculate your estimated operating expenses to arrive at net income.
o Examine hazards such as market saturation and legislation.

Strategic Pricing

Setting a sensible price for your Airbnb is essential if you want to increase revenue and attract visitors. There is no one-size-fits-all rate, but you may greatly influence the success of your investment by modifying your daily rate according to variables like the day of the week, seasonality, and market demand. To maximize your Airbnb pricing, take into account the following tactics:

o *Dynamic pricing*: Implement dynamic pricing techniques to have your prices automatically adjusted in response to rival pricing, current market demand, and other pertinent variables.
o *Seasonal modifications*: Adapt your price to account for variations in demand throughout the year. You might raise your prices to take advantage of increased demand during busy times of the year and on holidays. Conversely, you can draw customers by running specials or discounts during off-peak hours.
o *Weekend vs weekday rates*: Be aware that the types of guests and levels of demand may alter between weekdays and weekends. To attract midweek bookings, modify your rates appropriately, charging more on weekends and less on weekdays.

o *Discounts by length of stay*: Offer discounts for longer stays to entice customers to make longer reservations. Think about putting in place tiered pricing arrangements, in which visitors receive longer-term, gradually larger savings.

o *Competition analysis*: Perform regular competition analysis to stay up to date on pricing changes in your market. Keep an eye on comparable properties' rates in the neighborhood and modify your own rates to maximize profitability while staying competitive.

o *Value-added services*: Increase the perceived value of your listing by providing extra features or services like parking, Wi-Fi, or free breakfast. Make a price adjustment to account for the extra value you give visitors.

o *Guest Reviews & Feedback*: Keep an eye on visitor evaluations and comments to determine how valuable people think your listing is in comparison to rivals. Make adjustments to your pricing plan and take care of any areas that need work using the information provided.

A great way to accumulate assets that provide you with a steady stream of income is by investing in Airbnb rentals. A well-chosen acquisition may provide consistent cash flow and an asset that appreciates over time.

CHAPTER ELEVEN
DEALING WITH TENANT TURNOVER

Tenant turnover is one of the unavoidable difficulties you will have as a landlord or property management. When a tenant vacates your rental property, there is a vacancy that must be filled by a new renter. This is known as tenant turnover. Effectively managing tenant turnover is critical for maintaining a consistent rental income and keeping your property in good condition.

Tenants are informed by their landlords when their lease is about to expire. States have different require-ments for how much notice you must give; nevertheless, most regulations call for 30 or 60 days' notice. The tenant then chooses whether or not to extend their lease. In the event that the tenant decides to move out, the landlord will need to find a new tenant. You should look for a new tenant as quickly as you can. Your income decreases with each day the property remains unoccupied.

After that, a move-out check is carried out to make sure there are no damages and the house is in good shape. If the renter is liable for any damages, the landlord may deduct those expenses from the security deposit. But keep in mind you can never utilize the security deposit for typical wear and tear. The property can then now be advertised by the landlord. It could take some time to hear back from potential tenants, so don't worry if your house needs some upkeep in the meantime. The process of screening and viewing can always be scheduled for a later time.

The Turnover Process

Preemptive Planning

Handling tenant turnover begins long before a renter decides to quit. Planning ahead and putting in place procedures that make the process run more smoothly are the first steps. Planning ahead is the first step towards effectively controlling tenant turnover. Anticipating vacancies and preparing a plan will save you stress, time, and money. Establish a schedule for the handover procedure and budget enough for advertising, upkeep of the property, and any required repairs or improvements. By planning ahead of time, you may reduce downtime between tenants while maintaining rental income.

The following methods will assist you in maintaining organization and saving time:

- o *Maintain Good Relationships*: It is vital to maintain strong connections with tenants. You may extend the tenure of quality tenants by offering excellent service and attending to their demands.
- o *Regular Inspections*: Plan routine inspections of the property to spot maintenance problems early on. Taking care of these issues right away can help prevent expensive repairs and guarantee a smooth move-out procedure.
- o *Clear documentation*: Make sure all of your contracts and leasing agreements are clear and unambiguous. Tenant turnover issues can be avoided by having clear paperwork that minimizes misunderstandings and specifies expectations.
- o *Understand local laws*: Understand the rules and laws that apply to tenant-landlord relationships in your community. Being knowledgeable will make it easier for you to comply with legal standards during the transition process.

Giving Notice

Clear communication with your tenants guarantees that all move-out procedures are done right. Effective communication keeps everyone informed and helps to avoid misunderstandings. Here's how to have effective conversations when there are tenancy changes:

o *Prior notification*: Urge your tenants to notify you as soon as possible if they plan to move out. This minimizes any possible vacant periods by giving you plenty of time to organize and market the home for rent. As the day of their move-out draws near, politely remind your tenants. Giving them a move-out checklist and any other paperwork can help to streamline and manage the process for everyone involved.

o *Respond promptly*: To prevent delays, promptly address any questions or worries tenants may have regarding the move-out procedure. Even during times of turnover, maintaining a pleasant landlord-tenant relationship can be achieved by being accessible and approachable. You never know, maybe they'll get in touch with you again later on if they require a rental home. They might even recommend you to others.

o *Leverage technology*: Technology makes communication and paperwork much easier during this period. Simplifying the process overall, online portals or apps can be used to gather repair requests, arrange inspections, and exchange critical papers with tenants.

Streamline Pre-Departure Procedures

Make sure everything is in working order before your tenant vacates the premises. Prepare your rental agreement and make sure the tenant has followed all prior agreements.

o *Move out checklist*: Make a detailed move-out checklist that includes necessary items like cleaning, repairs, and utility transfers. To guarantee a seamless move-out procedure, give your tenants access to this checklist.

o *Conduct a move-out inspection*: To determine whether any repairs or cleaning need be done, you might want to arrange for a pre-move-out inspection with your tenants. This allows tenants to take care of any unresolved matters prior to leaving the property.

Preparing the Property

To reduce vacancy periods that follow the previous tenants, avoid wasting time and get the property ready for the next residents right away. To guarantee the quickest turnaround possible, observe the following tips:

o *Thorough cleaning*: Provide a cleaning checklist to the tenants so they may make sure they don't forget anything when cleaning. But it's essential to engage professionals to make sure the place is flawless for the next tenant. A spotlessly organized environment makes a good first impression on potential tenants.

o *Maintenance and repairs*: Examine the property to see what needs to be fixed or maintained. Before displaying the property to prospective tenants, take care of small problems like fixing leaking faucets, touching up paint, changing light bulbs, and making sure everything is in good working condition.

o *Cosmetic enhancements*: To update the appearance and increase the property's attractiveness, think about making little cosmetic changes. One way to make your rental property more appealing is to paint the walls, replace old fixtures, and repair or replace worn or damaged flooring.

o *Efficient scheduling*: In the interim between tenants, there might be a lot of upkeep, repairs, or even remodeling work. Make an effort to arrange these in a sensible order, and don't put off finishing them for too long. Make an effort to establish trusting connections with repair and cleaning providers. In this manner, you can work with them to efficiently coordinate duties and, in the event of an emergency or last-minute request, you might get their priority service.

Advertising the Property

Now that your previous tenants have departed, it's time to focus on the next critical step: locating your replacement tenants. Use a variety of media platforms to market your home in order to draw in prospective tenants. Capture stuning images, craft captivating descriptions, and emphasize the special qualities and advantages of the property. Listing your property on websites like Zillow, Trulia, and even Facebook Marketplace is something you can do on your own. Working with real estate specialists who can manage this on your behalf is another excellent strategy to increase your exposure. They frequently reach a far larger audience and have a pool of prospective tenants who are already looking for the ideal rental home.

Tenant Screening

Tenant turnover can have good effects as well because it offers you the chance to properly choose and screen your next tenant, despite its drawbacks. Don't rush the tenant selection process, even if it's crucial to keep your property occupied for as little time as possible. You don't want unqualified tenants to occupy your space. The following suggestions can help with tenant selection and screening:

o *Thorough Application Process*: Establish a thorough application procedure that includes employment verification, credit checks, background checks, and references from prior landlords. This gives you a good indication of the prospective tenants' qualifications.

o *Individual Interviews*: Conduct interviews virtually or in person as well. Ask pertinent questions, and pay close attention to what they have to say.

o *Clear expectations*: Make it clear to the tenant what you want in terms of rent payment, upkeep of the property, and other pertinent details throughout the screening process. This manner, prospective tenants are aware of your needs from the start.

Each tenant turnover allows you to examine and, if necessary, alter your lease agreement. Verify that the lease covers all necessary terms and conditions, such as the amount of rent, the date of payment, the length of the lease, the pet policy, and any additional guidelines or rules. To avoid further conflicts, take care of any concerns that may have developed with prior tenants.

Managing Property Transitions

During the spring, summer, and autumn seasons, more people tend to relocate. This implies more tenants arriving and leaving your property if you're a landlord. A well-thought-out plan is necessary for the smooth transition of a rental property between renters. A solid plan protects your investment, helps you find eligible tenants, and fosters confidence with potential tenants.

Moving out your previous tenants and bringing in new ones is a hard and exhausting procedure that can take a day or a week. Within a short time frame, furniture needs to be moved, keys need to be gathered, and damages need to be evaluated. Here are some pointers to assist make the procedure a little less intimidating and a little easier to handle.

Knowing everyone's schedule – Every tenant transfer is unique, even for seasoned landlords, and some will undoubtedly prove easier or tougher than others based on how much time you've provided yourself to manage all the required cleaning and checkups in between them. Maybe the new renters won't move in until a week after their lease starts. Perhaps the previous tenants had already moved out a few days before. It's also likely that they've procrastinated and haven't even reserved a moving truck for the day their lease expires. Find out from your tenants who is planning what and when in order to minimize the possibility of any unpleasant surprises. This will assist you in organizing your tasks so that no one is inconvenienced, and in anticipating any possible problems.

Clarify move-out instructions with tenants – Even the greatest tenants are unlikely to recall their lease by heart, and by the time their lease expires, there's no way they'll remember the specifics they agreed to when moving out. Make sure, well in advance, that your tenants understand exactly what is expected of them. Even cooperative tenants may become unhappy if you start offering them instructions when they are in the hurdle process of moving out. Things that seem obvious to landlords are not always obvious to others, so talk early and often when in question.

Get to know repairs in advance – Although landlord visits are seldom looked forward to by tenants, they are sometimes necessary when a lease is set to expire. Early detection of necessary replacements or repairs will save you a great deal of hassle throughout the tenant transition process. It is not appropriate for a group of new renters to move into an apartment with three bathrooms and discover that only one of the toilets is functional.

In fact, it's usually recommended that landlords do an annual inspection of their homes, preferably in the middle of the lease. Mid-term inspections guarantee that you discover any difficulties well in advance of move-out, including evidence of maintenance issues and lease violations. Don't put yourself in a bind by feverishly attempting to fix a leaking sink, damaged handrail, and nonfunctional shower the day before your tenants come in.

<u>Get it right with the new tenants from onset</u> – Even if you may want to sleep and get yours for three days by the time your new tenants are finally totally settled in, it is crucial to get things started correctly.

Ensure that, by the time you hand them the keys and send them on their way to furnish their new home, all of their questions have been addressed. Giving them little tips on the house's quirks can also be beneficial.

Perhaps you have to hold down the handle of the upstairs toilet in order for it to flush completely, or you have to elevate the doorknob a little to lock the backdoor. While these suggestions may not seem like much, they can be quite helpful to someone moving to a new home, neighborhood, or city.

Ensure you have trusted contractors – You'll probably be hiring someone to handle some cleaning and moving if you're not up to the occasionally Herculean effort of renovating an entire property. Whether you are searching through the phone book for a handyman or have been relying on one for years, make sure he will be there when you need him.

Transitioning renters will be much more difficult if you end up performing twice as much work as you anticipated.

Move-out inspection

When tenants move away, they frequently attempt to leave behind belongings. Anything they find difficult to move or decide they no longer want may be left behind. The removal and disposal of these objects will cost extra, particularly if they are big. Anything left over could also make it difficult for you to see any damage to the rental property. Giving tenants instructions on how to vacate is one approach to prevent this from occurring. Examine the house carefully and methodically as you make your way from room to room during the move-out. Jumping about could make you overlook something crucial. You might even extend an invitation to the tenant to come to the inspection, but if you think that having the tenant present will just lead to a hostile exchange, don't press the matter and instead conduct a thorough, well-recorded, and photographed move-out inspection.

Prior to the move-out inspection, educate yourself on your legal rights as a landlord. While some damages may be subtracted from the security deposit, you don't want to go beyond your legal bounds. Landlords cannot take "normal wear & tear" from a security deposit in the majority of states. Make sure you are aware of the financial obligations of your tenant when they vacate the rental property by researching tenant/landlord laws in your area with state and municipal authorities, your property management company or both. The rental move-out checklist is the best way to do the inspection. A sample checklist is available online or through a real estate or rental company. Make the checklist unique to your particular rental property and don't forget to add any unique agreements you have with the tenant, such as a pet waiver. To ensure you cover everything and record any issues you find, use a tenant move-out checklist.

Handling security deposit

Returning the security deposit too soon and then finding damages that should have been subtracted is one of the major blunders made by landlords. You have 30 days after the tenant moves out to repay their security deposit. Keeping the deposit unjustified is another typical error made with security deposits. Your lease agreement should ideally specify exactly what can be subtracted from the security deposit. Recall that this is not your chance to exact revenge on a tenant you didn't like. When it comes to the rental unit's particular conditions at the time of move-out, deductions from the security deposit must be justified.

If you intend to deduct monies from the security deposit, you must document the expenditures and work promptly to obtain estimates from contractors to settle any serious issues. If you plan to deduct money for cleaning or trash collection, you will also need to provide evidence of such expenditures. Within 30 days of moving out, you must contact the previous tenant to discuss the security deposit. Sending an itemized reconciliation is required if you are withholding all or any part of it. You may be responsible for three times the value of the initial security deposit if you don't reimburse the tenant or provide an explanation of the money you're withholding within thirty days of receiving the security deposit.

Importance of Move-In and Move-Out Procedure

Attracting a good renter is as simple as being a good landlord. If you own a multi-unit building, you may find yourself going through the move-in/move-out procedure on a regular basis. However, turnovers can only occur once or twice a year, or fewer, for landlords who own just one or two apartments. Maintaining organization is essential to making the transition seamless and free of errors.

Whether a tenant is switching from one rental to another or a long-term renter is leaving and a new tenant is moving in, successfully transitioning a rental property between tenants is critical. Effective transition management improves communication, shields you from unforeseen expenses and property damage, and establishes a positive working relationship with the incoming renter. It allows you and the tenant to get to know one another further and fosters trust.

It's during the move-in process that you get to know the new tenant. If you're lucky, you'll have the opportunity to meet the renter multiple times before they move into your building.

Initial actions that can establish a precedent include obtaining a security deposit and signing a lease. You want your tenant to understand how much you value your property and how much you prefer to maintain its appearance and upkeep.

Establishing the tenancy's ground rules is also necessary. The terms of your lease should include the amount of the security deposit as well as when and how it will be refunded. In order to avoid any misunderstandings, it is crucial that you and your potential tenant go over these clauses in the contract. It is important for your prospective tenant to understand that you will enforce fairness and legality, which implies that they must fulfill their end of the contract.

When the renter is ready to vacate, everything should go well provided that the landlord and tenant had a good working relationship from the start. Take a look at the move-out processes when the renter gives you notice. A move-out checklist will make it easier for you and the tenant to finish the required tasks without any problems.

Long-term Tenants Retention

Retaining current renters in rental property is far less expensive than finding new ones. Fortunately, there are strategies to reduce tenant turnover by enticing current renters to extend their lease. These are some tactics to promote long-term, amicable relationships with your tenants and encourage lease renewals.

Establish reasonable rent prices: Make sure your rates are competitive by keeping up with local rental pricing. Rent hikes that are reasonable can encourage tenants to stay. It's often advisable to only increase rent by modest amounts. You should also examine to see if there are any rent control mechanisms in place that limit how much and when you can raise the rent.

Consider offering incentives: If a renter chooses to extend their lease, you might wish to provide incentives. This could be a gift card, a reduction on the following month's rent, or a month's worth of free utilities.

Provide Extra Amenities: If you own a property, think about adding some appealing features or services. This can entail giving out free parking, installing energy-efficient appliances, or supplying high-speed internet. These extra features will make your property stand out from the others. Uncertain about the upgrades to make? Think about what will maximize your return on investment.

Provide responsive maintenance: Tenant-reported mainten-ance issues should be promptly resolved. By offering top-notch maintenance services, you encourage guests to stay longer by demonstrating your dedication to their comfort and happiness. They will also feel less irritated when everything works as it should.

Maintain consistent communication: Throughout their term, stay in contact with your tenants. Make sure you answer any queries or worries they may have right away. Moreover, you may think about sending warm welcome notes for the holidays, educational newsletters, or check-in messages to establish a relationship and make sure they feel appreciated.

CHAPTER TWELVE
MAXIMIZING PROFITABILITY

Owning rental property can be a profitable business, but maximizing earnings involves more than just collecting rent every month. Understanding the need of strategic financial management is not only useful to landlords, but it can also ensure that the earnings you receive at the end of the month are correctly managed.

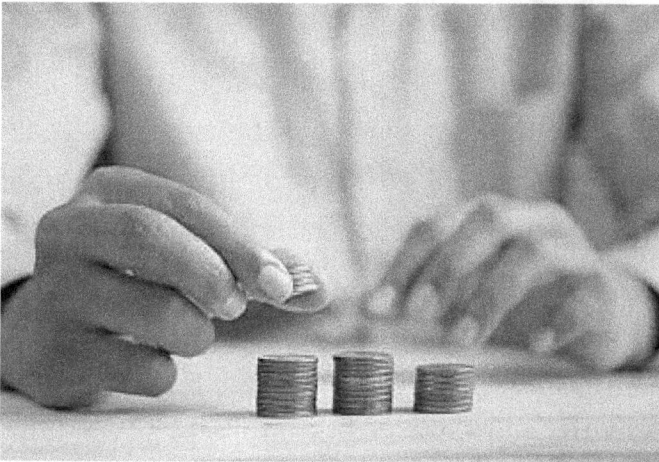

Efficient Budgeting

Efficient budgeting is a fundamental component of optimizing rental property earnings. In order to execute optimal budgetary techniques, landlords need to draft a thorough budget that accounts for both revenue and outlays. If you choose to do this yourself, you can begin by making a list of all possible sources of income, including monthly rent, late fees, deductions from deposits, and any other costs your tenants may have incurred.

Listing your expenses – Take into account both fixed and variable costs when calculating expenses. Whereas variable costs cover things like upkeep, repairs, and property management fees, fixed costs might include things like insurance, property taxes, and mortgage payments. An organized budget that gives a clear picture of the property's financial situation can be built on a strong foundation by beginning with a bill of costs. From this starting point, you may increase profitability by making well-informed judgments.

Income projections – The next step is to draft a document outlining every revenue stream your property may provide. Think about how much money your property brings in right now and whether there's anything you can do to raise the rent. This can involve providing your renters with extra amenities, parking spaces, or, if your poetry permits it, on-site recreational facilities. It is advisable to take into account the national economy and adjust your rental rate accordingly, taking into account financial trends such as inflation and overall market feasibility. By forecasting your prospective income, you may combine your profits and expenses to create a budget for property upgrades that will boost the rental rate.

Tax Strategies

Effective tax planning is an essential part of increasing rental property profitability. Most experienced accountants will advise landlords on various tax methods to improve their overall financial position in terms of rental income and profitability. As a landlord, you should take the following key considerations into account:

Depreciation: Accounting professionals will counsel you to utilize depreciation deductions for both the property and its various components. This tax plan can lower taxable income considerably. For landlords, depreciation is an essential topic in tax planning since it lets them recoup the cost of some improvements made to the property during its useful lifespan. Essentially, it is an annual income tax reduction that recognizes the property's natural deterioration.

Know Your Eligible Deductions – List all of the expenses that can be written off, such as maintenance expenditures, property management fees, and interest on a mortgage. Precise documentation of these costs guarantees proper tax reporting. A lot of landlords don't know about the deductions they can take advantage of, but qualified accountants can keep you informed about the most recent deductions that are acceptable as well as any expenses you can write off during tax season.

Investigate Applying for Tax Credits – An accountant can keep you up to date on available tax credits, such as energy-saving upgrades or low-income housing incentives. By making use of these credits, you may improve the property's overall financial performance and make sure that your profits increase without you having to pay large amounts of taxes when the time comes.

Expenses Tracking and Management

Meticulous tracking of expenses is essential for managing rental property income. Accurate financial reporting and analysis are crucial for filing tax returns and creating detailed budgets, and this may be achieved by putting in place effective systems for tracking and classifying spending. Here are some expert pointers for efficient rental revenue spending tracking.

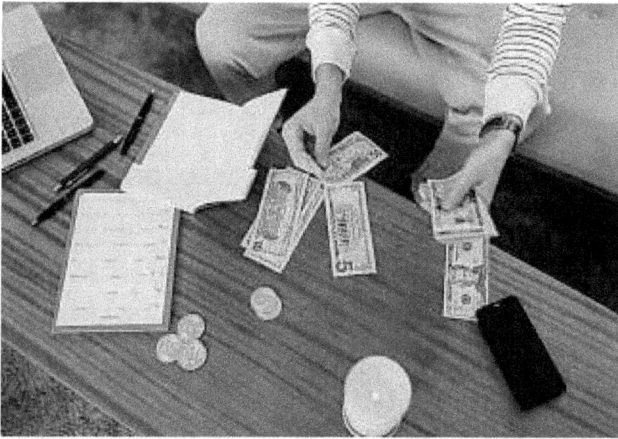

<u>Use Digital Tools</u>: You can collect all the information you need in one location and eliminate the need to keep track of a lot of papers and receipts by using accounting software and digital tools to expedite the cost tracking process. By automating data entry, these technologies can save time and lower the possibility of errors. The majority of accountants will advise using programs like Quickbooks or Xero because of their user-friendly interface and simple navigation.

<u>Improve Your Receipt Management Skills</u>: Keep a strict method for organizing and storing receipts. This is essential to guaranteeing adherence to accounting rules and supporting expenditures during tax audits. Receipt storage is facilitated by a number of digital solutions that are accessible to business owners, including landlords, and is particularly useful at year-end. It usually only takes you to take a picture with your phone and upload the receipt to a secure location for future reference, which makes filing and maintaining records much simpler.

Review Property Expenses Frequently: To stay on top of your outgoings and revenue, undertake regular expense reviews to find potential cost-saving options. These reviews are an excellent way to bargain with service providers, look into discounts for larger purchases, and determine whether or not recurring costs are really necessary. If you no longer require a service or if a better bargain is available, you can make the necessary adjustments. This is also an excellent way to keep the budget recent and your financial reports as accurate as possible.

Rent Adjustment Strategy

If you want to enhance your rental revenue, here are a few proven strategies that will help you achieve that:

Make Cost-Effective Upgrades and Improvements

Renovating a house from scratch or making expensive changes is not necessary if it is kept clean and well-maintained; doing so will simply reduce the amount of money you make in rent and long-term return on investment. But a few small improvements and modifications will give your house a new, contemporary appeal and let you raise the rent. Here's how to carry out renovations and modifications that increase rental values:

Focus on the Kitchen: Begin by ensuring that all of your kitchen appliances match. Your kitchen will appear sleek and contemporary when the finishes on your stove, refrigerator, dishwasher, and oven are all the same. If the appliances require frequent repairs or are old, you might want to install new ones. While you don't have to purchase expensive models, having energy-efficient appliances can make your home stand out to potential tenants, and stainless steel appliances will always raise the amount you can charge for rent. Renters are frequently prepared to spend extra for kitchen features like backsplashes, gleaming faucets, and smooth countertops. If you can only do one renovation to your rental home, let it be the kitchen.

Update Paint and Floor: Painting is a simple improvement that needs to be done whenever possible. Invest in higher-quality paint rather than the lowest one you can get. Though it's not necessary to invest a lot, well-designed walls will attract better tenants and higher rents. Tenants prefer hard-surface flooring to carpet. If it fits within your budget, rip up the carpet and put laminate or tile flooring in its place rather than buying new carpet. Even fake wood floors seem fantastic. These floors improve your rental value, are more aesthetically pleasing, and require less cleaning and upkeep. When your property is carpet-free, it always rents for more money.

Improve the bathroom: A warm and pleasant bathroom will distinguish your property from others on the market, attracting tenants ready to pay more for comfort and style. Some simple upgrades include installing a new toilet seat, changing the shower head to one with adjustable water pressure, and replacing sink and cabinet hardware. Make small upgrades that the tenants would value, such as adding storage space, and make sure the floors are clean and free of wear and scratches. Prospective tenants will notice a cupboard or storage over the toilet. Another thing that can help is a big, well-lit mirror above the sink.

Attract, choose and retain quality tenants
Tenant quality has an impact on your earnings. Renting to a qualified tenant will save you money, which will result in greater revenue even though you will still charge the same amount of rent to anyone who occupies your property. You won't have to waste time and money trying to collect past-due rent when you have a solid renter in place. After your tenant leaves, you won't have to be concerned about severe deterioration or damage to your property. There won't be any worries about broken leases or damage from pets.

Tenant retention also affects rental income. Tenants are more inclined to extend their leases year after year if they are happy in their house and think you're offering a wonderful rental experience. This implies more money in your pocket because you won't have to pay for turnover and experience vacancies. Make sure you respond to your tenants' requests for repairs. Express gratitude for timely rent payments and demonstrate your willingness to go above and beyond to make your tenants feel satisfied. Tenant retention is one of the best strategies to increase your investment property's earnings.

Give allowance for Pets
Pets generate additional money through pet fees and rent. Allowing dogs reduces the chance of vacancy and lowers turnover costs. Allowing pets in rental properties makes financial sense. It's a great approach to draw in a wider range

of possible renters. Actually, research indicates that 75% of tenants have pets. If you do not let pets into your property, you may face a lengthier vacancy period, which may cost you money.

When you allow dogs, you can charge a higher rent (by inputting pet rent) and potentially increase the value of the home. Pet deposits are another option. These will be paid for each pet, so if a tenant moves in with two cats, you will make several hundred bucks just by letting them stay on the property. Tenant quality is also frequently improved. Tenants that take good care of their homes are typically responsible pet owners. Encouraging pets in rental properties can be financially advantageous, provided that there is a clear pet policy and open lines of communication with the tenants.

By implementing these important methods and remaining proactive in managing your rental property, you may increase profitability, reduce risks, and achieve long-term success as a real estate owner. Owning a rental property may be a fulfilling

and successful endeavor with adequate preparation, invest-
ingation, and implementation.

About the Author

Donald E. Clay is a seasoned real estate investor and property management expert with over 15 years of experience in the industry. He began his career as a real estate agent, where he developed a keen eye for identifying profitable rental properties. Over the years, Donald has managed a diverse portfolio of residential and commercial properties, honing his skills in tenant relations, property maintenance, and financial management.

As graduate of Real Estate Studies, Donald is known for his practical advice and hands-on approach to property management. He has conducted numerous workshops and seminars, sharing his insights with aspiring landlords and seasoned property managers alike. His passion for educating others led him to write 'The New Landlord's Handbook' a comprehensive

resource designed to help new landlords navigate the complexities of property management with confidence and ease.

www.ingramcontent.com/pod-product-compliance
Lightning Source LLC
Chambersburg PA
CBHW071210210326
41597CB00016B/1752